D1461291

Made in BRITAIN

The Best of Quintessentially British Companies

JAMES FIELDING

summersdale

MADE IN BRITAIN

Summersdale Publishers Ltd
46 West Street
Chichester
West Sussex
PO19 1RP
UK

www.summersdale.com

ISBN: 1-84024-605-7
ISBN 13: 978-1-84024-605-6

Made in BRITAIN

The Best of Quintessentially British Companies

JAMES FIELDING

CONTENTS

Introduction

It all started on the Real Tennis court at Petworth House. There I was playing doubles when, probably in angst over another missed shot, I looked down at my racquet and noticed a small label: 'Made in England'. This wooden racquet that I viciously whack about the court every week was beautifully crafted somewhere in Cambridge.

And yet story after story was appearing in the press about British companies moving their manufacturing abroad – even companies that we think of as symbolically British. It set me thinking immediately about what else, apart from my tennis racquet, was still made in Britain. This is the birthplace of the industrial age, of great inventors and a proud manufacturing heritage that once employed so many. Was it all disappearing, or was there still hope? We see plenty of budding inventors and investors on the television these days, after all.

What I discovered over the course of my research, I'm happy to say, made me proud to be British.

I looked for a broad cross section of consumer products that might still be made here.

So many companies which have somehow survived amidst global competition were helpful in providing information about their business. What I found were human stories of passion, belief, hard work and determination over many years. It was also heartening to see new companies enjoying success in different areas and even resurrecting old factories, resolved to keep traditional methods and skills alive. While Britain may no longer have the huge textile factories and heavy industry it had in the early twentieth century, nor be able to benefit from the cheap labour available in other parts of the world, it is clear that British businesses have learned to adapt with the times, and their ingenuity and creative energy is unsurpassed.

Every time a product is imported into this country it has an impact on the environment. At a time when we are all aware of the need to minimise our carbon footprint, I hope this book will inspire you to look for areas where you can buy British, whether in the food you eat, the car you drive, the clothes you wear, your household furnishings or leisure goods. Moreover, so many of the companies in this book pride themselves on ethical business standards and practices and, above all, producing high quality items that are made to last.

Some of the companies within these pages have been built up over the last few decades, while others have evolved over centuries. Some create everyday products, others luxury items or highly specialised technology. Some have a handful of staff, while others are worldwide brands employing thousands. I expect there will be names you recognise and others you'll be discovering for the first time. The selection will arouse debate, arguments for what's in and arguments for what's missing. And perhaps it will inspire some readers to learn new skills or set up their own business.

Above all, I hope you enjoy reading about these companies as much as I enjoyed discovering them.

James Fielding

Thank you to all the companies who provided information and photographs in order to be involved with this book. *Made in Britain* contains no advertising, and inclusion in the book was in no way financed by the companies chosen, but was purely an editorial decision based on the information available at the time of research.

If you would like to tell us about other companies making products in Britain, please contact the author via the publisher at jamesfielding@summersdale.com.

For the Body

Daniel Prince

What they make:	bespoke jewellery
Founder:	Daniel Prince
Founded:	2002
Based:	Hatton Garden, London
Number of staff:	9 (six are part-time)

DANIEL PRINCE was first inspired to create his jewellery company when he was looking for an engagement ring for his wife. He noticed a large gap in the market – it was possible to buy high-end Bond Street designer jewellery or cheap, tacky products, but there was nothing available in between these two extremes. Unimpressed, he decided to buy his own diamonds and get the ring made specially, but found that the diamond business was extremely unhelpful to newcomers – no one was able to offer him advice on the cut or quality of the stone he should buy. He felt there must be room for a company that was more consumer-friendly; one that would be open and honest and help people to make an informed purchase; that provided Bond Street

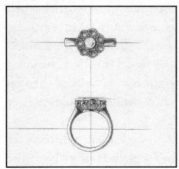

quality but without the designer label prices. And so Daniel Prince the company was born.

The company makes bespoke jewellery, designing unique rings tailored to customers' requests – perhaps incorporating stones that the customer already owns, finding jewels of a specific colour,

or coming up with an original or unusual shape for the setting. All their work is entirely handcrafted, and manufactured solely in the UK; unlike most other jewellery businesses, they use no imported, mass-produced components in their products. Rings are made using flat metal bullion, or hand-forged completely; while being shaped, the metal is constantly heated, re-filed and re-worked to get the best possible shape and quality. The stones are also fitted and polished by hand, so that their beauty and vitality is shown to perfection. This attention to detail is especially noteworthy when mass-produced imports mean that these techniques are in jeopardy. Although new, the company wants to encourage traditional jewellery-making techniques, and hopes to do this by expanding its workshop and training a new generation of jewellers, thereby ensuring that Britain's heritage of silversmithing and master craftsmen survives.

The company is based in historic Hatton Garden, which dates back to the fifteenth century; Sir Christopher Hatton built the largest house in Elizabethan England. Since the 1870s the Hatton Garden area of London has established its international reputation as London's jewellery quarter. The London diamond centre is at No. 100, where diamonds are 'fingerprinted'.

Daniel Prince create more than simply engagement rings. For instance, they can also make you a 'right hand' ring (a contemporary concept where a woman buys a ring for herself as a personal reward or to celebrate independence) or an eternity ring (usually bought for wedding anniversaries or the birth of a first child; traditionally, the stones are set within the structure of the ring rather than mounted above it) as well as diamond earrings, pendants, and a range of other pieces to commemorate key moments in your life. Daniel Prince also guarantee that their diamonds are 'conflict-free' by purchasing from legitimate sources not involved in funding conflict and in compliance with United Nations resolution – meaning no person is harmed in the process.

Interesting fact: Diamonds come in a variety of colours, including violet, orange and green. Red is the rarest.

Ede and Ravenscroft

What they make: ceremonial gowns (and wigs, in some cases) for legal, academic and regal occasions; tailored menswear

Founders: William and Martha Shudall

Founded: 1689

Based: Chancery Lane, London and Cambridge

THE COMPANY'S long and impressive history dates back to 1689, when the Shudall family firm of tailors was commissioned to produce coronation robes for William and Mary. The Shudalls were renowned for their craftsmanship and attention to detail, and with their shop located in what is now Aldwych, the centre of the tailoring trade, they were well-placed to make their mark.

They went on to create ceremonial robes for the funeral of George II, and then, in 1761, further robes for his son George III's coronation (not only those for the King himself, but for over a hundred peers too). William Shudall had died by this point, but his wife Martha continued to run the business until her retirement around 1770. Francis Stone, a robe-maker who had been running the firm in partnership with Martha, remained in power, and was appointed robe-maker to George III; as well as maintaining the company's position as robe-makers for the Knights of the

Most Noble Order of the Garter. (The firm now makes robes for six different orders of chivalry.) Francis died in 1797, passing the prosperous business to his son-in-law, William Webb.

Meanwhile, the Ravenscroft wig-making business, founded by Thomas Ravenscroft in 1726, was also thriving. In 1822 Thomas's grandson Humphrey managed to perfect (and patent) a horsehair wig that did not require powdering or curling – definitely a good thing, because before then the powder and ointment used for the daily treatment of wigs frequently damaged the wearer's clothing. Humphrey's template for a low-maintenance wig is still used today.

On Humphrey's death in 1851, his son Francis took over the business at the age of 22 – despite his youth, he was already the governor of Birkbeck College (now a constituent college of the University of London) and would remain so for the next 50 years. In 1811, William Webb's robe-making business took on an apprentice, Joseph Ede. Joseph's well-to-do uncle, Thomas Adams, purchased the firm in 1834 and it became known as Adams and Ede. Joseph was appointed robe-maker to William IV, and later, to Queen Victoria.

The two companies combined their strengths in 1871, when Joseph Webb Ede, son of the first Joseph and now owner of the business, married Rosanna Ravenscroft, granddaughter of Humphrey. Sadly, Joseph Webb died not long after at the age of 26, and Rosanna took over the firm – it would remain under female

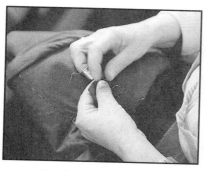

management for the next 60 years.

The firm became Ede and Ravenscroft in 1921. Ten years later Rosanna Ede died; she was commemorated by all the London papers, having held a royal warrant for over sixty years. But the company lived on — Elizabeth II was crowned wearing an Ede and Ravenscroft robe, and Ede and Ravenscroft was one of only eight companies to hold royal warrants for Queen Elizabeth, the Duke of Edinburgh, Prince Charles *and* the Queen Mother all at the same time.

Ede and Ravenscroft provides bespoke and tailoring services as well as a ready-to-wear-menswear department which includes ties, morning and evening tails, black tie and casual wear. Not only that, but it's almost certain that if you've graduated from a British university, you hired your gown from them. From coronation to graduation, from country pursuits to judicial robes — what could possibly be more British?

Interesting fact: Ede and Ravenscroft has produced royal garments for every British coronation since that of George III.

Edward Green

What they make: gentlemen's Goodyear welted shoes
Founder: Edward Green
Founded: 1890
Based: Northampton, Northamptonshire
Number of staff: 55

AS THE company themselves say, Edward Green seek to provide 'the finest shoes in England for the discerning few'. In our current throwaway culture, Edward Green promotes investing in a long-lasting, good quality product that will only improve with age, rather than buying cheaply and throwing away after a year.

The pieces that make up a pair of shoes are cut from a single small, fine calf skin and then prepared according to the style. For instance, raw edges are coloured, perforations and gimping or shark's tooth edging are added with an old hand-operated machine guided by eye. The pieces are then sewn together; Edward Green

is unusual in that the shoes start to take form at this stage, being assembled over a wooden block similar to their final shape, rather than the pieces being stitched together flat. The craftspeople work in teams; one fits the pieces together, the other sews. Machines are used at Edward Green when a suitable one exists to do the job but only when it doesn't reduce the quality. Eyelets are also put in individually rather than being drilled in a line, allowing for greater flexibility in positioning.

Edward Green use traditional wooden lasts (blocks that the shoe is pulled over to give its definitive shape) because these absorb moisture from the damp leather. The shoes are lasted in four steps using old machines with lots of hand adjustment rather than entrusting them to a single fully mechanised process. Once nailed into place they are left to dry. The longer the shoes are left for, the longer they will keep their shape in the future; Edward Green tries to leave them for three to four weeks.

Then the shoes are 'constructed'. The Goodyear welt is sewn to the upper. Goodyear welting describes this particular method of construction and is popular among British shoe manufacturers. The welt is a piece of leather which is sewn both to the upper and subsequently to the sole. At Edward Green the stitches are concealed beneath the sole of the shoe but can be seen running along the upper outside edge. Their accessibility means that they can be returned to the manufacturer who can remove the worn soles and rebuild the shoes as necessary, thus prolonging

their life for many years. Before attaching the sole, a wooden shank or stiffener is added beneath the arch and a layer of crushed cork which takes the form of the foot when worn, ensuring maximum comfort.

When the sole has been stitched to the welt, the heels are attached: they are built in layers by hand. Any rough edges are trimmed and hot wax is applied to both sole and heel to repel water and for colour.

Finally, the shoes are polished. Antique waxes are applied to make them look as if they have been well-loved, maybe even a little worn – and then the shoes are brushed and polished, again by hand. This process was invented by John

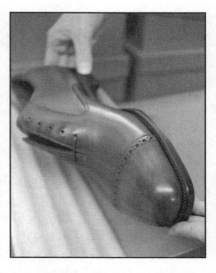

Hlustik, who bought the company in 1983, because he wanted the shoes to look as though his grandfather might have worn them.

Interesting fact: Hand-sewing on Edward Green shoes is performed using a pig's bristle, not a regular needle; this is because a pig's bristle is thinner and can be passed through a fine cut. Using a steel needle would make a hole in the leather. The sewing thread is made by the handsewer using four or five strands of a cotton-polycotton mix which is stronger than cotton alone. The thread is waxed and some of this wax is left in the cut during sewing and helps, like the fine bristle, avoid leaky shoes.

Geo F. Trumper

What they make: gentlemen's barber and perfume products
Founder: George F. Trumper
Founded: 1875
Based: Mayfair and St James, London
Number of staff: 50+

GEORGE TRUMPER established one of the first exclusive barbers and perfumers for gentlemen in London. The company is still based in the original 1875 shop, which retains much of its original style.

In the nineteenth century most men did not shave themselves; the well off were shaved by their servants, the not-so-well off would go to a 'penny barber'. Today it is a luxury to be shaved by someone else, but one that Trumper is happy to provide, as well as haircuts, tints, facial-hair trimming, manicures, pedicures and

chiropody, and massages. In addition to all that, they also run the world's first shaving school where barbers give one-to-one advice on how to shave, based on beard and skin type.

Trumper also make shaving brushes, all of which are made of badger hair; this hair absorbs water (as human hair does) and

it is soft enough not to irritate the face. The hair is taken from countries where badgers are not endangered or protected, but it is sorted and processed in England.

Trumper's hairbrushes and combs are all crafted in ebony or simulated ivory; the bristles are natural fibres to stimulate the scalp. The ebony is always taken from protected replanted forests.

Trumper also make use of naturally occurring goodness; for instance, they sell blocks of alum, a mineral stone sometimes purported to be the world's first aftershave because of its soothing properties; their violet shaving cream is suitable for sensitive skin due to violet's natural therapeutic characteristics.

Six monarchs, starting with Queen Victoria, have honoured Trumper with the royal warrant.

Trumper combines a twenty-first-century belief in the importance of male grooming with a nineteenth-century style, class and durability; in the meantime showing that it is possible to take pride in your appearance without harming the planet.

Interesting fact: The playwright Tennessee Williams was a fan, claiming that 'the very best hairdressings come from Geo F. Trumper'.

Gieves & Hawkes

What they make: shirts, suits, shoes and everything
else a well-dressed man needs –
including the socks, belt and braces
Founders: Gieves and Hawkes
Founded: 1771. The company was formed from
two famous businesses: Gieves was
founded in 1785 and Hawkes in 1771.
Based: Savile Row, London
Number of staff: 100

ALL OVER the world, Savile Row stands for the very best in
men's tailoring, and Gieves & Hawkes is Number One Savile Row.

Built in 1732 as the town
house for the Fairfax family,
then taken over in 1871 by the
Royal Geographical Society,
the address was occupied by
Gieves & Hawkes in 1912.
With world leaders, film stars,
musicians, businessmen and
royalty regular customers,
Gieves & Hawkes is a British
treasure with a long and
esteemed history.

Since 1809 when King
George III requested their

work, 200 years of unbroken royal service has ensued. One Sunday in the early nineteenth century, the Prince Regent sent a messenger to Hawkes requesting his immediate attendance. However, the cap maker was a religious man, and he sent the messenger back saying, 'Tell His Royal Highness that for six days I serve my King, on the seventh day I serve my God.' The Prince Regent took this rebuff in good part, and continued his patronage.

The battlefields of the world were also rather well-dressed in the eighteenth and nineteenth centuries. Both Admiral Lord Nelson and the Duke of Wellington sought out Gieves & Hawkes, experts in the tailoring of intricate naval and army uniforms, to create their dress. Records show that Nelson's Flag Captain Hardy, also a customer, took lodgings above the original shop in Portsmouth. The company despatched a steam yacht to the Black Sea in 1854, equipped with tailors among other resources, to sail with the British Fleet during the Crimean War. They went on to supply the military and ceremonial dress to numerous states around the world.

Prior to World War One, Gieves & Hawkes developed and patented the first inflatable life-saving waistcoat, which saved the lives of countless members of the armed forces and civilians. An original version, which saved the life of a Lord Montague, is now on display in the Beaulieu Museum, Hampshire.

In 1926 they released their first limited set of ready-to-wear men's garments and continued to diversify, all the while improving and perfecting the bespoke tailoring for which they are famous. All their ready-to-wear garments are designed and conceived at their headquarters, and most are made in Britain; they use non-British resources only when the finest quality materials can not be found in Britain. Today Gieves & Hawkes make formal evening wear, casual wear and suits.

The Gieves Sea Chest, which first received the approval of the Admiralty in the middle of the nineteenth century and remained in great demand until the 1930s, was fitted out with all the necessities for a naval cadet or officer including clothing, shaving bowl with mirror and clasps for telescope and dirk. An original is still displayed at Number One Savile Row, the company's headquarters and flagship store. There are a further 22 stores and concessions in the UK, and fine stores and concessions in China, Hong Kong, Taiwan, Japan, Dubai, Turkey, Russia and Ireland, all offering the very best in quality materials, design, craftsmanship and service.

Interesting fact: 'Dr Livingstone, I presume?' It could hardly have been anyone else. David Livingstone and Sir Henry Morton Stanley were both dressed and equipped by Gieves & Hawkes for their central Africa expeditions.

Grenson Shoes

What they make: shoes
Founder: William Green
Founded: 1866
Based: Rushden, Northamptonshire
Number of staff: 80

WILLIAM GREEN was born in 1835, and when he was four his recently widowed mother moved with him to Rushden in Northamptonshire. This county had always been a good spot for shoemakers; it had forests to provide oak bark and charcoal needed for tanning, grass plains for the cattle who yielded hides, and water to wash the hides and, later, to provide power. But shoemaking was still a cottage industry; William learnt to make shoes first by helping his mother at home, and then, after he'd moved out in 1860, worked in his own home.

Such shoemakers used middlemen, known as factors, to sell their products; the factors would obtain orders, source materials, allocate work to the craftsmen and handle the finances. However, when demand dropped, a few factors ended up controlling most of the industry, which meant uncertainty and often hardship for the shoemakers. William and his mother had experienced this, and so when William became a factor in 1866, he made the unusual decision to draw up a formal contract for the shoemakers to do business with his newly formed company, William Green & Son, thus attracting the best shoemakers. His products soon became famous for their consistently good craftmanship and high-quality materials. Soon

William was able to open his own factory, Green's Yard, in 1874.

By the time William died in 1901, the company had moved to larger premises in Queen Street, which soon had to be expanded due to increased demand. It was realised that making the company's products more distinctive would increase demand still further, and so the Grenson brand name (a contraction of Green and Son) was introduced in 1913.

During World War One, Grenson's focus moved to military-issue shoes, but then returned to civilian shoes. During the stock crashes of the following few years, Grenson managed to honour all contracts even if this meant making a loss – but it was also decided to try and make the Grenson brand more upmarket. This turned out to be a wise choice – Grenson survived the Depression with relatively little damage when over half the shoe manufacturers in Northamptonshire went bankrupt. Grenson also developed a range of made-to-measure shoes which sold at lower prices than the bespoke shoes offered in London.

During World War Two, the factory again focused on footwear for the military; in this case, naval and flying personnel – including a pilot's boot with a pocket to hold a commando knife. If a pilot was shot down, he could use the knife not only for defence but to remove the top part of his boot, leaving only the shoe and making him less detectable.

After the 1950s, shoes became far more popular than boots. Manufacturing techniques also changed, although Grenson still handcraft the majority of their shoes. But with their new Rushden Range, a younger collection that's around half the price of their main selection, and over fifty stockists for it, they are able to remain in the forefront of shoemaking, appealing to a new generation of customers.

Interesting fact: The 'Grenson' brand name was one of the first to be registered in the UK.

Kent Brushes

What they make:	a wide variety of brushes for hair and body
Founder:	William Kent
Founded:	1777
Based:	Hemel Hempstead, Hertfordshire
Number of staff:	30

THERE ARE very few UK hairbrush manufacturers left; most are imported. G. B. Kent, or Kent Brushes, as they're more commonly known, are not only the longest established manufacturer of hairbrushes in the UK, but still use a wide variety of traditional techniques to make their products; they are the only company in the UK still producing handmade bristle brushes.

One of the oldest established companies in Great Britain, G. B. Kent and Sons was founded by William Kent, who, it is said, delivered his products using a string of pack horses. From these

modest beginnings the company flourished, and by the 1820s it was providing toothbrushes for King George IV. As history marched on, Kent went from strength to strength; it received a Medal of Excellence and royal appointment to Queen Victoria in 1851, and the factory moved to larger premises for the first time – not surprising, as it was apparently producing over eight and a half thousand bone-handled toothbrushes every week. The April 1874 British trade journal commented that 'Messrs. Kent and Co may be justly regarded as the representative firm of the brush making industry', and by 1882 over 600 people were working there (of both genders; the females apparently 'picked for the pleasing feature of comliness').

Display a KENT stand ... and sell *Quality !*

"Allure" PERFUME HAIRBRUSH ALSO MEN'S MODEL

A KENT Display Stand is the Hall Mark of *Quality and Service!*

In 1900 the company became public and moved to Farringdon Road, where it would remain until 1940, selling brushes to ironmongers, chemists, silversmiths and many other professions all over the world. In 1901 it also built factories by the River Gade in Hertfordshire; timber and coal were transported along the water and unloaded at the factory's own wharf, as well as raw materials from all over the world, including exotic woods, badger hair and whalebone.

Kent continued to serve the British public during World War One, providing seven different types of brush for the War Office – including special toothbrushes for Indian troops that contained no pig bristle or bullock bone due to religious reasons. It was also one of the first companies to use a motorised delivery van – a 24 horsepower 'commercial car', bought in 1908.

After the wars, Kent's fortunes declined somewhat, and on the death of the last Kent brother, Arthur, the company was acquired by Cosby Brushes, a family-run business. The Cosby family still own the company today, with four family members working full-time at the factory. Kent's cheapest brush is a handbag brush for £4.95, but they still produce a completely handmade brush which

retails at £99 – not surprising, as it can take up to 540 hours to produce just one. After shaping, drilling, sanding and lacquering the wood for the base, the bristles are then stitched by hand into the head of the brush. Boars' hair is used for the bristles; it is a natural protein whose success at removing unwanted chemicals and products from the hair can't be reproduced with synthetic fibres. Each brush is then carefully checked for any faults before brass screws are added by hand.

Despite the time spent on each brush, Kent manages to produce one million hairbrushes and over half a million handmade combs each year. The bristle is sourced from the finest merchants in India and China, while timbers are chosen from sustainable forests throughout the world. Kent's objective is to provide every conceivable brush needed to care for and style hair; they now have a range of over 250 brushes and combs, including shaving, make-up, styling, exfoliating, travel, tooth and nail brushes. Certainly they are not afraid to embrace the future, and they are still managing to hold to the principles which have done them proud for the last 225 years. They claim to be the world's finest brush-maker; clearly they must be doing something right, because at a time when many British brush companies have fallen by the wayside, Kent remains strong and hopeful for the future.

Interesting fact: During World War Two, Kent Brushes concealed maps and compasses in their shaving brush handles so that escaped British prisoners could find their way home using them. Creation of these brushes was carried out in a locked, windowless room at the factory and only a few employees were allowed in.

Kinloch Anderson

What they make: highland dress
Founder: William Anderson
Founded: 1868
Based: Edinburgh, Midlothian
Number of staff: 30

WHAT COULD be more Scottish than a kilt? Kilts are, as Kinloch Anderson say, 'a symbol of pride and brotherhood' and their history can be traced back to at least the end of the sixteenth century; tartan has been around possibly since the seventh century. With this in mind, Kinloch Anderson's reputation for providing traditional Scottish dress means they are well-deserving of a place in this book.

Tartan had been banned after the Jacobite Uprising in 1745, and the ban was not lifted until 1782. But after George IV chose to wear tartan on a visit to Scotland, interest in this traditional cloth rose, and when Queen Victoria had her own personal tartan designed (none but the royal family may wear it) its future seemed assured – and the boom in popularity meant

that an aspiring tailor called William Anderson decided to turn his business into a limited company in 1868. Kinloch Anderson was born.

By the end of the nineteenth century, the company had become known as Scotland's premier tailors for civilians, and in 1903, it first supplied clothing to royalty – King Edward VII, as it happened. By the time World War One began, Kinloch Anderson had also branched into military tailoring, creating officers' uniforms for all the major Scottish regiments.

In the 1930s, Kinloch Anderson took the then very daring step of introducing ready-to-wear men's clothing to its line – something most reputable tailors would have been shy of doing. However, it paid off, because in 1934 the company received its first royal warrant, from George V, and thrived as other clothing businesses declined. The company's chairman visited Canada in the 1950s and its wholesale division was established; by the 1970s, they were able to start marketing their high quality ladies' skirts to Japan. Kinloch Anderson had also been appointed tailors and kilt-makers to both Queen Elizabeth and the Duke of Edinburgh by this point and, in 1980, the Prince of Wales was added to this list.

The company is currently headed by the sixth generation of the Kinloch Anderson family and, in addition to its wholesale and bespoke Scottish dress, also provides tailoring advice and exclusive tartans for corporations. The Kinloch Anderson brand has been developed widely under licence in the Far East and there is a second brand aimed at the younger man, Kinloch², which is very popular in South Korea. Whenever there's an appropriate occasion for a man to don a kilt, Kinloch Anderson will know about it and be able to offer advice on everything from how high above the knee to wear your kilt to what tie to wear if you're getting married in traditional Scottish dress. Kinloch Anderson offers the widest range of kilt options available and says that their kilts frequently become family heirlooms.

Interesting fact: If you do not have a clan tartan associated with your name and Scottish family heritage, district or region, you can still wear one of the universal tartans: the Black Watch, the Hunting Stewart, the Caledonia and the Jacobite.

Launer

What they make:	handbags, wallets and other leather goods
Founder:	Sam Launer
Founded:	1941
Based:	London and Walsall, West Midlands
Number of staff:	18

SAM LAUNER, a refugee from Prague, arrived in England over sixty years ago. It was his home country that taught him one simple idea; handbags and other leather goods should be elegant, made from the finest materials and created by skilled craftspeople. These ideals are still aspired to today; all Launer goods are handmade using calf, lizard and ostrich skin.

Skins are specially tanned for Launer and cut, often by hand, to ensure that only the most blemish-free areas are used. The cut parts are then skived and split, a technique that refines and thins the edges of the leather. The leather can then be turned so that no raw edges will show on the finished product.

The leather parts are then fitted together by hand, craftspeople working with sewing machinists to ensure a perfect result. Every item is inspected at each stage. A lot of Launer's employees have been with the company for many years – the factory in Walsall is headed by Gary Barnes, who has worked for Launer since he left school.

The current managing director, Gerald Bodmer, also leads the design team, travelling around Europe to spot key design trends. Gerald started off in another leather goods company which held the royal warrant to the then Queen (now the late Queen Mother) but eventually left and set up his own company before arriving at Launer in 1981. The company was producing a lot of pieces for Gucci at the time, but when Gerald arrived he altered the company's ethos, focusing more on putting together in-house designs to produce a range of own-brand goods.

There are only about half a dozen leather goods manufacturers left in the UK, but Launer are certainly ahead of the game when it comes to high-profile customers. The Queen awarded the

royal warrant to the company in the 1960s for handbags (yes, Launer is responsible for one of the Queen's most instantly recognisable personal symbols). In 1991 she visited the factory, and the following year Launer was awarded the royal warrant for other leather goods as well. They recently created a handbag for the Queen to mark her eightieth birthday.

Launer sells its products in Great Britain to well-known stores such as Fortnam and Mason, Harrods, Pickett and John Lewis, and it also exports to Japan, Korea, Hong Kong and Singapore. The brand has featured on Japanese TV, and Crown Princess Masako of Japan has bought Launer bags. She is in good company – the Duchess of Cornwall, Dame Judi Dench, Baroness Thatcher and the late Diana, Princess of Wales, have all purchased Launer handbags in the past, making them vital accessories to some of our most famous English icons.

Interesting fact: Launer's managing director used to be the principal clarinettist of the Carl Rosa Opera Company.

Luke Eyres

What they make: made-to-order school, university, college and sports wear; college scarves and starched collars
Founder: Mr L. Eyres
Founded: 1894
Based: Cambridge, Cambridgeshire
Number of staff: 9

LUKE EYRES has displayed a marked ability to adapt with the times. In the early part of its existence, a major chunk of its output was black lisle stockings, which formed a key part of women's attire during the late nineteenth and early twentieth century. From the early 1900s to the end of the 1920s, the company produced traditional pullovers, and during World War One supplied balaclavas and gaiters to the British troops.

Due to wartime shortages, there was not enough wool yarn to create knitted college scarves, so the company decided to develop a woven wool material, leading to the distinctive vertical striped style of college scarves today. After the war ended, wool became widely available again,

DOUBLE BLUE
Luke Eyres
Since 1894
Made in Cambridge, England

but most universities elected to keep the cloth stripe style. The scarves were mainly made for Cambridge Colleges and boat clubs, but soon became popular with universities all over the UK. The company realised a potential market lay before them and began making cricket sweaters for colleges, incorporating a different trim for each institution. Luke Eyres sweaters ended up being worn by all the major cricket teams including MCC, the West Indies and Yorkshire.

1989 saw the introduction of the company's first electronic machines, which allowed it to branch out into the school wear market as well as to perform fashion work for Paul Smith and

Joseph. It was one of the first companies to use a pearl binder machine, and also one of the first to develop with their supplier shrink-resistant yarn to allow people to machine-wash their clothes.

And now, in the twenty-first century, Luke Eyres has added yet another product to its list – it is one of the few companies in the world to make stiff collars for a range of legal, military and social occasions. The collars are produced entirely in-house; made from the finest cotton, they are first heavily starched, then dried and polished – this last step is carried out using hundred-year-old, gas-fired machines.

Collars and scarves are currently the object of the company's focus – the scarves are also traditionally made using original manufacturing techniques. Luke Eyres provide scarves to many higher education institutions, both in the UK and overseas; it possesses a definitive library of scarf designs, among which are nearly all British universities and colleges. This library has been preserved and updated for two centuries. College-style scarves have also been becoming popular as fashionable accessories, and a number of leading international fashion houses have included Luke Eyres scarves in their seasonal collections.

From courtrooms and cutting edge fashion houses to cricketing and Oxbridge, Luke Eyres has helped define the style of some of our most famous British institutions.

Interesting fact: Luke Eyres has produced items for Burberry, Paul Smith and Joseph among other high-profile names.

Neal's Yard Remedies

What they make: complementary health and beauty products
Founder: Romy Fraser
Founded: 1981
Based: Covent Garden and Gillingham, Dorset
Number of staff: 180

IT IS an amazing and indeed quite frightening fact that 60 per cent of what we or the environment puts on our skin ends up in our bloodstream. From shampoo to sunscreen, nail varnish to lipbalm, fake-tan to moisturiser and every product in between, be

it cream, oil, paste or spray, much of it ends up coursing around our veins. Wouldn't it be sensible, then, to use natural products?

Over the last 50 years thousands of new chemicals have been created. It is impossible to avoid all these chemicals but we can minimise contact by using only naturally found ingredients in the products we use on our skin and hair. Neal's Yard Remedies help to make that possible.

When the company was set up in 1981 by former teacher Romy Fraser, Neal's Yard Remedies was one of the few companies pushing against the synthetic approach to skin and health care that was the norm at that time. The aim was to create an outlet to provide a focus for increasing awareness and acceptance of complementary health and beauty therapies; to take away man-made chemicals and sell a completely natural product.

The first shop opened in Neal's Yard, Covent Garden in London, stocking an extensive range of essential oils and homeopathic remedies, and well-informed employees were available to assist customers in their selection, encouraging them to take responsibility for their own health and well-being. A range of skin and haircare products was developed utilising the beneficial effects of herbs and essential oils, packaged mainly in the now familiar blue glass bottles.

A stop at Neal's Yard is now on the itinerary of many tourists whilst in the Covent Garden area. Neal's Yard Remedies have expanded with 30 stores now in the UK and 10 in Japan. They also operate over sixty therapy rooms alongside their shops, where leading independently-qualified practitioners offer everything from Indian head massage to homoeopathy and acupuncture consultations and treatments.

The company recently opened their own eco-factory and headquarters at Peacemarsh, in Gillingham, Dorset, where they make natural and organic health and skin products to make us look and feel great. They offer the largest range of Soil Association certified organic health, skin and body care products in the UK. All packaging is completely recyclable and all sourced products are GM free. Moreover, none of their products are tested on animals, only human volunteers. They support fair trade and build and maintain healthy working relationships with growers of exotic herbs worldwide including growers in the Amazon rainforest, Tanzania, Tamil Nadu, while most of the English herbs used in the products are grown organically on site.

It is a simple idea that lives up to our new ideals of clean, chemical-free products.

Interesting fact: Stars of film, fashion, politics and music swear by Neal's Yard Remedies, from Bjork and Uma Thurman to Johnny Depp and John Malkovich.

Norfolk Lavender

What they make: lavender-scented bath and shower products, lavender oil and accessories for home and garden
Founder: Linn Chilvers
Founded: 1932
Based: King's Lynn, Norfolk
Number of staff: 50 (20 part-time)

'ENGLISH LAVENDER' is often used to refer to the variety of lavender *Lavandula*, which is in fact grown and distilled to produce lavender oil all around the world – but there's no confusion about Norfolk Lavender's products, all of which are made using lavender grown on the family farm in Norfolk.

The company was founded by Linn Chilvers, a botanist's son with a keen interest in lavender plants. In 1874, he started a nursery garden and florist's business on the north Norfolk coast, growing several varieties of lavender. He carried on the

business after his father died; he had always been keen to grow lavender on a large scale, and so decided to try it in Norfolk, which provided satisfactory conditions for growing the plant (as opposed to the south of England, where many lavender fields had failed). In 1932, he went into partnership with Francis Dusgate, aka 'Ginger',

who was able to provide six acres of land for Linn to grow his 13,000 plants. Four men – well, three men and a boy – planted the crop, taking 18 days to do so, for a total cost of £15. The first harvest was in 1933.

The venture had attracted much publicity, and came to the attention of a Mr Avery, a chemist from London. He was able to provide Linn with a recipe for lavender perfume that had been made for King George IV, and for many years he came to Norfolk to manufacture the perfume himself; when he died, the company purchased the recipe, the beginning of their expansion into a wider range of products.

In 1978 the company took several steps to become more consumer-friendly and to educate visitors about its processes. An old miller's cottage was converted into a tearoom and the stills were moved to a building next to the drying barn. People could now witness the distilling and visit the fields.

By the 1980s the company was producing 60 products and exporting them to more than twenty-five countries, as well as selling them in over 500 places around Britain. A modern warehouse had to be built behind the distillery, and Caley Mill, the original production area, was converted into a gift shop. In the 1990s, the company tapped into the growing interest in essential oils and aromatherapy, offering jasmine, lily of the valley and rose oils; it now also offers a mail order service. Clearly they're on the right track; in 1977 there were only ten permanent members of staff, plus 12 to assist in the summer season, whereas now there are 50, which shows just how much the business has thrived.

So, is English lavender oil the finest in the world? English lavender distillers have always had a good reputation, for two reasons; firstly, because of England's climate, they have had to select the best, hardiest plants, and also tended to plant single varieties rather than seedlings. Secondly, England is at a higher latitude than various other lavender-oil-producing areas such as the south of France or Tasmania, so the longer summer days and cool noons remove the more volatile elements of the oil, making it pleasanter and less sharp. You could clearly do worse than buy British in this case; and if you pay a visit to Norfolk Lavender's farm, you will not only be supporting UK industry, but you'll learn a whole lot more about how the product is made.

Interesting fact: If Norfolk Lavender's rows of lavender were planted in one long row, they would stretch from Heacham, Norfolk to Hyde Park Corner, London.

Swaine Adeney Brigg

What they make: umbrellas and leather goods
Founders: James Swaine and Thomas Brigg
Founded: 1750
Based: London

THERE ARE two things you can be sure of in life. One is taxes, the other is that it will rain in Britain. It rains at the most inconvenient times, too; on our lunchbreaks, on birthdays, on Friday night when we are just about to go out and of course on bank holidays. But that is why we invented umbrellas and it is quite apt that some of the finest umbrellas are made in Britain. Such is the prestige and quality of the umbrellas made by Swaine Adeney Brigg that they make them for the royal family, by royal appointment.

Swaine Adeney Brigg has a complex and long history that dates back over 250 years, during which time they have developed an extensive range of leather goods including luggage, attaché cases and brief cases. Their famous Gladstone Bag, so called as it was the favourite of the former British prime minister, is a style symbol in itself. All

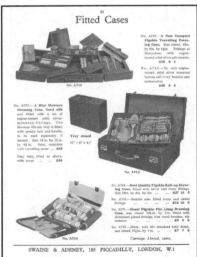

of the attaché cases, document cases, luggage and umbrellas are still produced in their Cambridgeshire workshops using the same crafting skills as were employed when the company began. All of the hides used are from domestically reared animals and are finished by hand and fed with tallow and oils, resulting in the most durable English bridle hide.

In 1750, John Ross founded a whip-making business at 238 Piccadilly. James Swaine purchased this business in 1798, having for some years been foreman of a successful whip-making business in Holborn. Swaine was something of a master of his craft and word of his leather expertise soon reached the upper echelons of royalty. Appointments to His Majesty King George III and to his sons, the Prince of Wales and the Dukes of York, Clarence, Kent, Cumberland and Cambridge followed. Swaine Adeney's reputation for excellence in leather goods was established, and they exhibited to the world at the London Exhibition held in the newly constructed Crystal Palace in 1851, winning several prize medals. They went on to exhibit their fine goods at the Paris Exhibition in 1900.

Thomas Brigg and Son's was established in 1836 at 23 St James's Street, a stone's throw from Swaine Adeney Brigg's present historic location, handcrafting the finest umbrellas, walking sticks and hunting crops. The store became a bastion of elegance to the dandies of the day who could not be seen in London without a fine umbrella. Thomas Brigg and Son's became, in 1893, the first umbrella-maker to be honoured with royal appointment.

It was during World War Two, when Brigg and Son's lost its Paris shop after France was occupied, that the two companies were brought together. It was February 1943 when Swaine Adeney Brigg & Son's Limited, as it is known today, was formed.

Brigg umbrellas are still all handcrafted with burnished woods, sterling silver nose caps and handwoven silks – as the company says, 'more of an art form than an item for rain protection'. The most popular and famed umbrella is the one-piece construction, usually made from the stronger woods such as oak, maple or hickory. The whole umbrella is fashioned from one single block of wood from handle to tip and oozes British heritage. No self respecting City gent should be seen without one.

Interesting fact: They used to produce a sword umbrella by request, as made famous by Jon Steed in *The Avengers*, and the original James Bond attaché case as seen in the film *From Russia with Love*.

The Celtic Sheepskin Company Ltd

What they make: sheepskin footwear, clothing, soft-
furnishings and car accessories
Founded: mid 1970s
Based: Newquay, Cornwall
Number of staff: 35

THE CELTIC Sheepskin Company started life as the Original UGG Co. in the mid-1970s, making the now famous UGG boots and other assorted leather goods.

In August 1990, Nick and Kath Whitworth bought the company and in 1991 registered the term UGG as a UK trademark. Five years later they sold the UGG name and renamed their company The Celtic Sheepskin Company Limited; while they still made

boots cut to the same pattern, they would now be sold under the Celtic Sheepskin brand name. The company has steadily expanded to become one of the largest mail-order suppliers of sheepskin footwear and clothing in the UK. They have also been trading online successfully for over nine years, building a substantial customer base in the UK and overseas.

Their traditional range of hard-wearing, fashionable footwear is designed, manufactured and distributed from their factory in Cornwall. The Celtic Sheepskin Company's gentle nourishing skincare products, luxurious scented candles, mohair socks and woollen blankets are all sourced in Cornwall and made in Britain. Although not all of their products are made in Britain (they also work with organic-cotton farmers in Uganda, paying above the market price and contributing to a non-profit-making British charity, Rock of Hope, to benefit farm-holding communities there), they support and work closely with British manufacturers to produce a wide range of high quality sheepskin outerwear and accessories. They are members of the Real Sheepskin Association which includes tanners, merchants, designers, manufacturers, retailers, specialist aftercarers and other trade institutions within their membership. The Association is dedicated to supporting young designers.

The Celtic Sheepskin Company wants their products to be good for their customers, the environment and for the production workers. For the first time they have been able to source recycled wool, resulting in less pollution, reduced water and energy use. This new product range will be introduced in their new catalogue, printed on FSC (Forest Stewardship Council) certified paper thereby supporting the growth of responsible forest management worldwide.

They have recently signed up to the Royal Mail's Carbon Neutral Delivery Service, which allows Companies to compensate for their CO_2 emissions by investing in environmental organisations or projects such as wind farms, solar installations or other energy efficiency projects, or through activities such as planting trees.

The Celtic Sheepskin Company are working towards their objective of minimising their impact on the environment – to prove that it is possible to produce excellent products, at reasonable prices, with a clear conscience.

Interesting fact: UGG-style boots originated in Australia and were used by surfers to warm their feet after spending long hours in the sea. The Australian and Cornish surfing fraternity have always had a close relationship and eventually, in 1973, the boots were introduced to Newquay in Cornwall.

Vollers Corset Company

What they make: corsets
Founder: Harry Voller
Founded: 1899
Based: Portsmouth, Hampshire
Number of staff: over 30

CORSETS – ORIGINALLY a vital piece of underwear for all properly-brought-up ladies, then a key weapon in the sex kitten's arsenal and now a stylish and original high-fashion concept for many special occasions. Vollers Corset Company have adapted with the times and their future has never looked so good.

The company was founded in 1899 by Harry Voller, who, living in the maritime city of Portsmouth, had ample chance to

observe the navy and decide that he didn't want to have anything to do with it. Once he'd finished his education, he got a job with Totterdell and Sons, a corset company based in the area, before founding his own business with his wife, Nelly, also a corsetière. They ran their new corset shop from their single-fronted home in Kingston Road. Records from that time show what Harry had to purchase to get his show on the road: needles for a few coppers, suspenders for sixpence, whalebone for seven shillings, lamps and oil for two, and coal for five. He also paid an assistant one shilling a week. By the end of the first week the company had taken one pound, two shillings and nine pence, but... well, see the interesting fact below.

However, in 1905 Nelly started her own corset company, trading under the name of Madame Voller, and the Vollers were able to move

MADAME VOLLER'S : :

: *Straight-Fronted Corset.* :

No. 501.   A splendid shape for full and medium figures.

White and Dove - - - Price **8/11**
Fancy Brocades and Black - - „ **10/6**
Including Two Pairs Suspenders.
Made to Measure, 2/- Extra.

across the street to bigger premises, including a first-floor factory. Madame Voller's made a range of corsets, including a 'closed back' corset 'specially designed for Ladies who are subject to colds in the back' and a 'Hercules' corset 'fitted with "Hercules" unbreakable steels'.

The business was handed down to Harry's son, and from him to Harry's two grandsons. They worked together until World War Two, when one went off to fight; on his return, one son focused on the shop, the other on the factory. The latter sadly became ill with a brain tumour and was unable to continue; he had been running his part of the business on a much smaller scale, with just six factory employees working three days a week.

However, in 1991, Ian Voller, Harry Voller's great-grandson, took over the business with his wife Corina. Ian handles day-to-day running and direction of the business, while Corina focuses on design.

Thanks to Madonna's iconic use of the corset, business has been steadily growing since Ian took over the company, and although the Vollers shop in Portsmouth has closed, Vollers supplies corsets to several high-profile stockists, including Figleaves, the largest online lingerie store in Britain, and Selfridges.

So, whether you want a corset to show off to that special someone, to wear to a party, or even just to pull your waistline in, you can buy from Vollers safe in the knowledge that your purchase has been made with care and attention and you are supporting British tradition – even if that tradition has been altered since Harry Voller first opened his shop. In a world where clothes are often made thousands of miles away from where they'll be sold, Vollers corsets show that it is possible to be ethical *and* sexy.

Interesting fact: During its second week of business, the company took no money at all.

Food and Drink

A. E. Rodda & Sons

What they make: Cornish clotted cream
Founder: Alfred Ernest Rodda
Founded: 1890
Based: Scorrier, near Redruth, Cornwall
Number of staff: 90

DURING THE first half of the nineteenth century the mines in Cornwall produced up to two thirds of the world's copper. Gradually, however, the prosperity of the mining industry began to subside, and miners had to open their eyes to other ways of making a living. One such miner, Thomas Rodda, looking for a home for his family, purchased the tenancy to a farmhouse in the remote location of Scorrier and set about making clotted cream. The house he bought still stands overlooking the factory, as testament to the humble beginnings of the business.

It was his son, Alfred Ernest, who first established the name of A. E. Rodda. Initially, milk from the family-run farm was turned into clotted cream and merely sold to friends and neighbours. The milk was left to stand in an enamel pan and then gently heated on a Cornish range until the cream on the surface started to clot. Left to cool overnight, the clotted cream was then skimmed off the surface. Cornish clotted cream is still the same; a luxuriously thick spooning cream, with a unique golden crust and a silky smooth texture.

The nineteenth century brought tourism to the South West and with it came the Londoners who wanted this most decadent of creams in their homes and shops. This set the Rodda family thinking, and in 1924 experiments bore fruit. They realised that by sterilising the cream and packing it into preserving jars, the cream could be kept for longer than the usual two to three days. Since the 1950s Rodda's have developed new ways of increasing the shelf life of a fresh product, perfected freezing techniques and introduced insulated pots for posting, ensuring total quality assurance in health and hygiene. Today that means they can supply nationally to supermarkets, caterers, corner shops, restaurants, pubs and tearooms, as well as exporting as far afield as Hong Kong. You can even enjoy a Rodda's Cornish Cream Tea flying at 30,000 feet when it may be served as part of the onboard flight menu.

Although machinery is now used to carry out the process, and the milk comes in tankers from across the county, this creamy delicacy is made in fundamentally the same way today as it was over one hundred years ago. Since 1998, Cornish clotted cream has been protected under EU food law. The Protected Designation of Origin award means Cornish clotted cream can only be made in Cornwall with Cornish milk and to a traditional recipe. It is British companies like A. E. Rodda who are keeping alive the rich heritage of the UK's traditional foods. They are also makers of rich, golden butter, liquid cream and delicious crème fraiche.

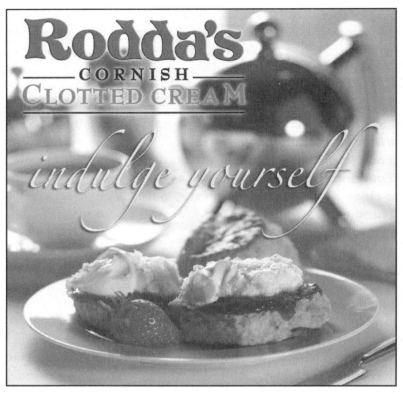

Clotted cream is naughtily indulgent and can be eaten with a whole host of foods, adding a taste of luxury to scones and strawberry jam, fresh strawberries, Christmas pudding and pies. The Rodda family recommend trying the Cornish delicacy 'Thunder and Lightning' – home-made bread with a good dollop of clotted cream and streaks of golden syrup laid over the top.

Interesting fact: Clotted cream was once described by former British prime minister Lord Gladstone as 'the food of the gods'.

A. G. Barr plc

What they make:	soft drinks
Founder:	Robert Barr
Founded:	1830
Based:	Cumbernauld, North Lanarkshire
Number of staff:	over 1,000

IF YOU grew up in Britain, chances are you partook of an A. G. Barr product many times in your youth. IRN-BRU, TIZER and the range of returnable glass bottle Barr flavours including limeade, ginger beer and cream soda... all have a place in the nation's heart.

The original Barr family business actually began as a cork cutting operation, founded by Mr Robert Barr in 1830. However, things started to go downhill when technology moved on to more modern ways of sealing bottles, and so his son, also Robert, started a soft drinks business in 1875 in Falkirk, supplying the local population

with 'aerated waters'. His son, Robert Fulton Barr, then set up another soft drinks business in Glasgow in 1887 but after five years he left for Ireland and the business, which was passed on to his younger brother Andrew Greig Barr, became A. G. Barr & Co. Ltd in 1904. The original Robert Barr enterprise continued to trade in the east of Scotland

but in 1959 A. G. Barr & Co. Ltd bought it, forming one family business. The company's current chairman Robin Barr is the fourth generation of the Barr family who have headed the soft drinks business and the Barr family continue to have a substantial shareholding in the company.

By the early 1960s the combined company operations had seven branches in Scotland, and had already taken its first steps across the border in 1954 when it bought John Hollows of Bradford. Further buyouts in the 1960s, 1970s and 1980s included Tizer Ltd in 1972 and Mandora St Clements in 1988, and in 1996 the company entered the water market for the first time with an investment in Findlays Natural Mineral Water. More recently, in June 2006 Barr acquired the Strathmore Spring water business which draws its water from the Vale of Strathmore at Forfar, Scotland.

In 2005 work began on developing the company's Cumbernauld site; £24 million has been invested in its development into one big facility containing production, warehousing, distribution and a new head office block. The highlight of the site's distribution operation is a new high-bay warehouse; it's tall as a cathedral with a height of 14 pallet bays, and it can hold over 12,000 pallets.

So... what about that IRN-BRU? Well, since its launch in 1901 it has gone on to become the number one grocery brand in Scotland, and it's one of the top 100 grocery brands in Britain. When it was created in 1901 it was sold under the name of Iron Brew, with the sporting personalities of the day endorsing the drink; for instance, in 1905 or thereabouts, Alex Munro, undisputed champion wrestler of Great Britain and world champion caber tosser, said, 'Barr's Iron Brew was a splendid tonic while training and a grand pick-me-up after a tussle...'

Iron Brew became the company's leading brand during the 1920s and 1930s but raw material shortages which developed during World

War Two caused the British government to effectively nationalise the industry in 1942; all branded drinks were replaced by six standard flavours. Barr's Iron Brew was therefore off the market, but in 1946 the company were looking forward to being able to sell it again. However, proposals for new food labelling regulations were being put forward which would make it illegal to sell drinks with misleading names... which was a problem for Iron Brew, because although it did contain

0.125 mg of iron per fluid ounce, it wasn't actually brewed. The company decided to trademark the phonetic spelling IRN-BRU and market the drink under that name upon its reintroduction in 1947. Heavily advertised (from the comic strip *The Adventures of Ba-Bru and Sandy* running from the 1930s to the 1970s – making it the longest-running commercial cartoon in history – to the slogans 'Made in Scotland From Girders' and 'Your Other National Drink' in the 1980s) the brand became ever more successful and has been joined by both Diet IRN-BRU and, in 2006, by an energy variant, IRN-BRU 32. Chairman Robin Barr and one other board member are the only two people in the world to know the recipe for IRN-BRU – the identity of the other board member is also kept secret.

Andrew Greig Barr died from glanders virus at the age of 31 in 1903, never living to see the progress of the company which bears his name. However, for over a century his company has stood up masterfully to the competition within the industry, still producing unusual, distinctive brands – and still manufacturing in Britain.

Interesting fact: Most soft drinks contain only one flavour; IRN-BRU, A. G. Barr's leading brand, was launched in 1901 containing 32.

Davenport Vineyards

What they make:	wine
Founder:	Will Davenport
Founded:	1991
Based:	Horsmondon, Kent and Rotherfield, East Sussex
Number of staff:	5

AFTER TRAINING in oenology at Roseworthy College in Australia and gaining further experience in the vineyards of France, California and Australia, Will Davenport planted a six-acre vineyard in the rolling countryside of Kent in 1991. Since then Davenport vineyards have gone on to be one of the most respected wine producers in England, increasing their vineyards to over 19 acres in Kent and East Sussex and producing around

15,000 bottles of white and sparkling wines every year.

They favour aromatic grape varieties, including ortega, faber, bacchus, huxelrebe, siegerrebe and pinot noir. Their flagship wine is the Limney Horsmonden, a regular award winner in the UK Vineyard Association annual wine of the year competition, and the sparkling Limney Estate quality sparkling wine is made from 55 per cent pinot noir and 45 per cent auxerrois and aged on lees for over two years.

What makes Davenport special is their commitment to organic farming and growing, which they see as a science as important as the holy grape itself. It was decided in 2000 to turn manufacture into a completely organic process. Davenport are extremely proud that their vines are not subjected to synthetic chemical fungicide sprays or insecticides, while the vineyard soil is not treated with weed killers and the soil fertility is not maintained by the addition of chemical fertiliser compounds.

The only pests that are not eradicated by the natural processes and natural life existing in the vineyard are wasps and birds. Birds are controlled by meticulously netting the entire vineyard during the growing (after failed attempts to use bird scarers). Wasps are dealt with in a similarly organic and scientific way – jam and sugar in jars. (Not honey, as this would attract and harm the bees.)

Although still a relatively small and young business, Davenport is rapidly becoming a leader in English wine, often commented about in the wine press as one of the most innovative, pioneering and consistent of the English vineyards. As interest in home produced, organic, environmentally friendly products increases, Davenport will strive to remain one of the UK's finest. Says Will Davenport: 'I don't really want to expand, as I prefer to keep my role hands-on… We only export to one buyer, the British Embassy in Greece. Every year the Embassy in Athens buys ten cases of English wine, which they serve to Greek officials with fish and chips.'

As long as there are devoted, talented English wine growers and distillers like Davenport, the industry will thrive. Cheers!

Interesting fact: Davenports Vineyards were chosen as wine supplier to the Millennium Dome.

Dickinson & Morris

What they make: pork pies
Founder: John Dickinson
Founded: 1851
Based: Melton Mowbray
and Leicester, Leicestershire

IN THE 1760s, around the time the Earl of Sandwich first put meat and cheese between two slices of bread to keep his hands clean at the gaming table, pork pies were mainly eaten by peasants. By the 1790s, the Dickinson family were already well known as pork pie-makers and Stilton cheese merchants. As the 1800s saw Nelson at the Battle of Trafalgar and Charles Darwin set sail for the South Seas, here at home fox hunting centred on Melton Mowbray, with three hunts favouring the surrounding countryside. The gentry discovered that small hand-raised pork pies were ideal as a cold snack during the hunt as they remained intact in their pockets.

As stagecoaches began to stop in Melton Mowbray en route to London and Leeds, it became possible to sell pork pies outside the immediate area. When the railway line opened, the fox-hunting gentry could now find their favourite snack in London. In 1848, John Dickinson opened his first shop at Burton End, moving to larger premises in Nottingham Street in 1851. He hired Joseph Morris in 1886 as an apprentice, and in 1901 the business took on the name Dickinson & Morris. Dickinson & Morris is now the oldest remaining baker of the authentic Melton Mowbray pork pie in the town centre today.

In 1992, after fire had devastated their period-style building, Samworth Brothers bought the property and carried out extensive refurbishment and renovation in conjunction with English Heritage. Ye Olde Pork Pie Shoppe reopened in October of that year. In response to the high demand for Dickinson & Morris pork pies nationwide through leading high street retailers, the baking of these pies now also takes place at a bigger bakery located just outside Leicester.

How do they make the authentic Melton Mowbray pork pie? The pastry is hand raised; filled with the finest fresh (uncured) pork, coarsely chopped, and a secret blend of spices; sealed by hand; and baked until golden brown. Once cool it is filled with bone-stock jelly, and wrapped in parchment. Melton Mowbray pork pies have a distinctive 'bow-walled' shape which is the result of them being baked without the support of a hoop or tin. This requires a very special type of pastry. They have a high meat content and no hydrogenated fats or artificial colours, flavours or preservatives.

Continued demand for such quality products led to Dickinson & Morris opening a sausage shop next door, offering a wide variety of premium speciality sausages. As a means of keeping all their passionate customers happy, Dickinson & Morris have also established a chilled mail order service. Soon after celebrating the 150th anniversary of pork pie making at the Nottingham Street shop, Dickinson & Morris received the Gold Award for Outstanding Customer Service from the English Tourism Council, and the Gold Great Taste Award. Premium ingredients, time-honoured recipes and attention to detail have made the Dickinson & Morris name what it is today.

Interesting fact: Mary Dickinson (1768–1841, grandmother of John Dickinson), a noted pork pie-maker, is credited with being the first to use a wooden dolly to raise a pastry case: she is considered the originator of the hand-raised Melton Mowbray pork pie.

Fuller Smith & Turner (Fuller's)

What they make: beer
Founders: John Fuller, Henry Smith & John Turner
Founded: 1845
Based: Chiswick Lane South, London
Number of staff: over 3,000 (including staff at the company's 360+ pubs) across London and the South East

'YOU CAN'T be a real country unless you have a beer and an airline,' said Frank Zappa. There are over 500 independent brewers in the UK, not including the thousands of home brewers. As a nation, we like beer. And as the real ale renaissance continues, Fuller's is at the forefront, manufacturing some of the finest beer in the land.

One thing Britain has always been great at is combining water, malt, hops and yeast into beer – completely different from continental lager – *real* beer, dark and full bodied, with real flavour, brewed in casks. All Fuller's beers are brewed with pride and passion in the Griffin Brewery, Chiswick, London. Because all the ingredients are natural, their character can vary from year to

year, so no beer will be exactly the same every time it is brewed. Fuller's uses a longer maturation period than other British ale brewers – up to two weeks. During this time a small amount of yeast is introduced to start a secondary fermentation, which gives more rounded flavours to the beers, as well as greater stability – giving you a more consistent pint.

Records show that some form of brewing has taken place on the Chiswick site for 350 years. From the original brewery in the gardens of Bedford House on Chiswick Mall, the original company expanded and thrived until the early part of the nineteenth century, when money problems forced the owners, Douglas and Henry Thompson and Philip Wood, to seek a partner. John Fuller, of Neston Park, Wiltshire was approached and in 1829 he joined the enterprise and before long took over the brewery. In 1845 his son, John Bird Fuller, was joined by Henry Smith from the Romford Brewery of Ind & Smith and his brother-in-law, Head Brewer John Turner, thereby forming Fuller Smith & Turner. Descendants of those first partners are still heavily involved in the day-to-day running of the company.

Over the years Fuller's has built up a reputation for brewing outstanding beers, for such brands as London Pride, ESB and 1845. Since CAMRA (Campaign for Real Ale) first held their Champion Beer of Britain competition, Fuller's have won Beer of the Year five times. London Pride is Fuller's flagship beer, smooth and complex, and at 4.1 per cent ABV in cask, believed by Fuller's to be 'England's most sought-after session-strength premium ale'. It has been supported by a powerful advertising campaign whose theme is, 'Whatever You Do, Take Pride.'

Some say that brewing is the world's second oldest profession. Every great scribe has had something to say on the matter and more than a few of them will have had Fuller's British nectar flow over their lips at some point in time.

Interesting fact: Cask beer is live when it goes out to trade, meaning that a small amount of yeast remains in the cask. Because of this, storage conditions are crucial, and the brewer relies on the expertise of the licensee to store and serve the beer well.

Hovis

What they make:	bread, flour
Founder:	Richard 'Stoney' Smith
Founded:	1886
Based:	Windsor, Berkshire
Number of staff:	6,100 (British Bakeries),
	7,700 (whole Bread Bakeries Division)

HOVIS, ONE of the leading brands in baking, was the first bread company to include the benefits of wheatgerm in their bread and the first to take advantage of television advertising. The 1973 television advert *Boy on a Bike* was recently voted in a survey the favourite advert of all time. Throughout the last 60 years of

television, Hovis has launched television campaigns to promote healthy eating, with slogans such as 'Get Something Good Inside', 'Better Today Than It's Ever Been' and the most recent 'Hovis Is For Life'.

Richard 'Stoney' Smith was a miller who perfected a method that steam-cooked and thus preserved wheatgerm in bread without losing any of the nutrients from it. Knowing he was on to a winner, he went into partnership with Thomas Fitton and when they patented the brand in 1887, Fitton's mill went into production of 'Smith's Patent Germ Bread', a name that would prove difficult to market. Realising this, in 1890 Fitton and Smith launched a competition to find a new name for their brand. The winner, one Herbert Grime, came up with the name Hovis, derived from the Latin phrase, '*Hominis Vis*' meaning 'strength of man'. In 1898, with some 5,000 bakers now producing Hovis bread, the Hovis Bread Flour Company Ltd was formed in order to move their brand into a more public domain.

Ever since its conception, Hovis has tried not only to provide a product superior to its competitors', but also to encourage healthy eating amongst the British public. Every brand of their bread, from white to granary, is free from artificial preservatives and flavourings. Hovis has also strived to encourage kids to eat healthily, with their 'Best of Both' range, a white bread with all the wheatgerm goodness of wholemeal and more recently by the introduction of Invisible Crust, a bread uniquely baked without any visible crusts, which means kids eat the whole slice and none of the goodness is wasted. Hovis also manufactures several ranges of baking goods such as flour and yeast for baking in the family home.

Having recently celebrated 120 years in the business, Hovis is as strong today as it was all those years ago and is still just as dedicated to providing healthy, affordable bakery products for everyone in the UK.

Interesting fact: The 1973 Hovis television advert, *Boy on a Bike*, was directed by Ridley Scott, and Bill Maynard, who played the baker, went on to star as Claude Greengrass in *Heartbeat*.

Innocent Drinks

What they make:	smoothies and fruit-based drinks
Founders:	Richard Reed, Adam Balon and John Wright
Founded:	1998
Based:	London
Number of staff:	187

IN THE corporate, cut throat world of business, 'innocent' is a word often brandished but rarely adhered to. But when, in 1998, three Cambridge graduates and close friends went to a jazz festival in London to sell their home-made fruit smoothies, they did so with

honesty and a genuine desire to do the right thing. They wanted to quit their day jobs as well, but that was only so they could help make the world a slightly better place; 100 per cent naturally of course.

The story goes that the day after the jazz festival, Richard, Adam and John all quit their jobs and, with one month's wages in the kitty, set about creating the Innocent brand. All the smoothies were home-made and 100 per cent natural, hence their brand name, and within nine months (after some initial problems, doubt and financial conundrums) they were off. They rose rapidly to market leader and trendsetter (not just in fruit smoothies but also in marketing), and drive to continually push the boundaries of what a fruit drink company can be. Innocent now command a 65 per cent share of the domestic market and are setting their sights on global domination.

It is not only their good business sense, their desire to cement Innocent as a great British brand that can transcend product placement and marketing but also their work for charity and the environment that puts Innocent ahead of the field.

Good Samaritans are alive and well and they live in Fruit Towers somewhere outside of London. As well as making products that are good for you, they procure ingredients ethically, use ecologically sound packaging, reduce and offset carbon emissions across their entire business system, and give 10 per cent of profits annually to charities in the countries where their fruit comes from.

As they say, 'It all sounds a bit Miss World, but we want to leave things a little bit better than we find them.'

Interesting fact: All the fruit they use is imported by boat or rail rather than by air to reduce carbon emissions.

Mackays Ltd

What they make:	jam, marmalade and preserves
Founders:	the Mackay family
Founded:	1938
Based:	Carnoustie, Scotland
Number of staff:	100

MACKAYS BEGAN life in a small factory in Thistle Street, originally a carrot-processing plant. However, the factory was near the local berry fields, and the Mackay family saw an opportunity to move into preserve-making. They bought the factory and ran the family business until 1970, when they were bought out by United Biscuits and started supplying Jammy Dodgers.

Current Managing Director Paul Grant bought out the Mackays division of United Biscuits in 1995; at this time, Mackays was close to shutting down, had 19 employees and an annual turnover of about £1 million. However, Paul realised that Mackays had several things going for it – it was the only marmalade producer left in the Dundee area, it bordered Scottish berry fields and it still used traditional manufacturing methods, which gave its products a unique 'homemade' taste.

The company had no export sales, and Paul could see a missed opportunity there. He made exporting a priority, and today the company, which now has 100 employees and an annual turnover of almost £7 million, exports regularly to 26 other countries. Its products are especially popular in Japan. It has also won a slew of awards, including 28 Great Taste Awards over the last three years, and was one of only two UK food manufacturers to be given the Queen's Awards for Enterprise: International Trade in 2004. The company now has two brands: Mackays produces everyday jams and marmalades for grocery shops and supermarkets, and Mrs

Bridges makes luxury products for hamper companies, department stores and independent retailers.

Mackays is one of the last remaining companies in the world to make jam and marmalade using traditional 'open pan' slow boiling methods, crucial to giving the jams their homemade flavours. The fruit and sugar are slowly boiled in steam-heated copper-bottomed pans – this allows the natural pectin and acids to be released prior to setting. Unlike in automated factories, pans can be used to cook a different type of fruit from day to day according to demand. Mackays is the largest producer in Europe still using these methods.

Wherever possible, Mackays uses fruits from local Scottish berry fields and farms; the only exceptions to this rule are ingredients such as oranges and apricots, which must be imported. Scotland's temperate climate means that the fruit grows for longer and so has a richer flavour. Mackays has removed E-numbers, sodium and genetically modified materials from all its recipes – all its products are 100 per cent natural. It has also developed special recipes for when the customer or market requires a change in fruit content.

Mackays also makes lemon and lime curd, chutneys and relishes, honey, mustard and fudge, and a number of distilleries allow it to use their whiskys in its marmalade. The company certainly isn't afraid of trying new things: among its products are strawberry preserve with champagne, pink grapefruit marmalade, and pineapple and mango salsa. With creative ideas that appeal to customers all over the world, Mackays' future seems assured.

Interesting fact: United Biscuits converted the original Mackay family factory into premises for supplying the fillings for Jammy Dodgers in the 1970s.

Marmite Ltd (part of Unilever UK)

What they make: Marmite
Founders: George Huth and Frederick Wissler
Founded: 1902
Based: Burton on Trent, Staffordshire
Number of staff: about 200

MARMITE IS so ubiquitous today that it is hard to believe that the raw ingredient for it – brewer's yeast that had been used to ferment sugars into alcohol – was originally regarded by brewers as a waste material. However, three scientific discoveries – that the yeast was made of tiny cells, that the cells were actually living plants, and that it was possible to concentrate, bottle and eat the cells – changed this perception for ever, and also gave us one of Britain's most iconic foods.

The Marmite Food Company (later Marmite Ltd) was set up in Burton on Trent in 1902 with the ambition of putting the concept of bottling the yeast into practice on a commercial scale in the UK. Success was by no means assured: other similar enterprises in continental Europe to popularise the use of yeast extract had failed, and the company got off to a rocky start when they discovered that brewing methods used for continental yeast did not work for its British counterpart, necessitating several alterations

and additions to their machinery. But by 1905 the company was well on its way to success, foreseeing 'a steady increase in business' in its shareholders' report. In 1907 the company expanded to London, as Burton on Trent did not provide enough raw material for demand to be met; however, in 1954, the London branch of the company was moved back to Burton.

When Marmite was first placed on the market, it was perceived to be nothing more than a useful culinary adjunct, but in the first quarter of the twentieth century, substances which were then described as accessory food factors and which are now known as vitamins came to light, and Marmite was found to be a rich source of the group of vitamins now known as the Vitamin B complex. This massively increased demand for it, not only in Britain but all over the world, especially in India, Africa, Malaysia (then Malaya) and other places where malnutrition was prevalent.

The basic production method has changed little since Marmite was first invented. The used brewer's yeast is broken down to release soluble amino acids and proteins. This soluble material is then concentrated and filtered a few times before going through a unique (and top secret) process for flavour development. The end result is yeast extract paste – nearly Marmite but not quite. Finally, an extra blend of vitamins and vegetable and spice extracts are added to create the unique Marmite taste.

Images © Unilever UK

Thanks to its high Vitamin B content, Marmite did its bit for the UK in two world wars. In World War One it was included in soldiers' ration packs, and also became a staple food in hospitals and schools. During World War Two, Marmite became a dietary supplement in prisoner-of-war camps. And more recently, in 1999, it was sent to British peacekeeping forces in Kosovo after requests for morale boosting were received from the field.

In short, it is clear that from a humble little fungus – for yeast is classified as such – which was formerly regarded as so much waste, a valuable product has evolved, which has travelled much further than could have been foreseen.

Interesting fact: Marmite is a French word, pronounced 'marmeet' and meaning a stew pot or stockpot. The product Marmite was originally used to make and enrich soups, stews and casseroles.

Montezuma's

What they make: chocolates
Founders: Helen and Simon Pattinson
Founded: 2000
Based: Birdham, West Sussex
Number of staff: 50

HELEN AND Simon Pattinson, the husband and wife team behind Montezuma's, followed a dream of a lifetime when they gave up their jobs as City lawyers and travelled to South America. Disillusioned with a money-driven life, they sold their Putney

house, put their possessions in storage, and took off for an adventure among new landscapes and cultures. It was in Argentina that they first thought about the exciting opportunities the chocolate industry could provide, when they found a town with a large German settlement that included several excellent chocolate shops. Shortly thereafter, they accidentally found themselves staying on a cocoa plantation in Venezuela and became interested in how the high-quality cocoa was produced. When they returned home, they were so in love with the concept of owning a chocolate shop that they opened their first one in Brighton in 2000.

They have seven stores nationwide with hundreds more retailers successfully selling their chocolate around the UK. With over 250 products in the range, Montezuma's are keen to experiment with new recipe ideas, and aren't afraid to try unusual combinations, such as 'sweet paprika and strawberry' and 'orange and geranium'. 'We have never been scared of experimenting and listening to our customers,' says Helen Pattinson. Don't fear, though, if you prefer the more traditional bars such as Brazil nut or ginger. They never compromise on ingredients. Chef and restaurateur Rick Stein has called Montezuma's chocolate 'food obsession at its best'.

They are also passionate about their ideals. Most of their chocolate is organic and all of it is free from GM ingredients. They obtain their cocoa from co-operative plantations in Peru and the Dominican Republic and strive to ensure that their trading fairly approach is complied with to the highest standard. Among many environmental policies they recycle all their packaging and cardboard, re-use hot water used to melt the chocolate and they have replaced all the aluminium in their packaging. So successful has this been that they won an environmental award for their factory in West Sussex. And after all that, they still have time to do something for charity. Every year, Montezuma's stores support charities local to their areas by donating money and also organising fund-raising events, thereby getting involved with their communities. As one of their guiding principles states, 'Business is a force for great social influence and change and that we should meaningfully contribute to local, national and international communities with whom we trade.'

Montezuma's are proud to be an award-winning British chocolate-maker, creating much of their chocolate range by hand. Montezuma's is responsible for some of the most delicious chocolate in Britain and is known for superior products that keep customers returning again and again. Says Helen: 'Since the first moment on the first day of the first shop, we saw the reaction of our customers to the small range of chocolates and knew we had done something right and the risk was worth it.'

Interesting fact: Montezuma, otherwise known as Motecuhzoma Xocoyotzin or Motechuhzoma II, was an Aztec Emperor who loved chocolate.

Nyetimber Ltd

What they make:	sparkling wine
Founders:	Stuart and Sandy Moss
Founded:	1988
Based:	West Chiltington, West Sussex
Number of staff:	around 40 with seasonal variations

ALL RIGHT, so you like the idea of buying British, but right now you could be thinking there are some things you can't do without. How about wine? Everyone knows that the best wine isn't made in Britain… or is it?

The earliest record of the Manor of Nyetimber is in 1086, when it was noted in the *Domesday Book*. The house has passed through many hands, from the Cluniac Priory of Lewes to part of Henry VIII's grant to Anne of Cleves, but it has always had excellent conditions for producing sparkling wine. The greensand soil is well drained and the slopes are sheltered and many face south. Geologically, the area is similar to the Champagne region in France, and tends to have mild springs and warm summers (usually) which allows the three varieties of grapes Nyetimber grows – Chardonnay, Pinot

Noir and Pinot Meunier – to ripen to optimum levels. So, after searching for a locality ideal to rival Champagne, Sandy and Stuart Moss bought the house and grounds.

Nyetimber's first vintage, Nyetimber 1992, was widely acclaimed when it went on the market, and the company went on to win the International Wine and Spirit Competition Yarden trophy in 1998 with its second vintage, the Classic Cuvée 1993. The company has gone from strength to strength and won the same trophy again in 2006, along with the award for English Wine Producer of the Year.

In March 2006 the company was bought by wine enthusiast Eric Heerema. Under his direction, a large number of new vineyards have been planted, bringing the total area to 259 acres. Currently it produces, on average, 60,000 bottles a year, but with the increased plantings it is hoped that production will increase to 500,000 bottles a year.

Nyetimber sparkling wine is made in the same way as high quality vintage Champagne. Nyetimber's grapes are harvested by hand every October and taken to their wine press – imported from Epernay, it can hold four tonnes of whole bunches at each pressing, and is one of only about thirty such presses in the world. The juice produced from each pressing is then placed in stainless steel tanks, and kept separate according to vineyard site and grape variety. The must – that is, the juice containing pulp, skins and stems of the grapes – is fermented, on average for 12 days, to produce all the different base wines. These are studied through careful tasting trials and the results help Nyetimber choose blends or 'cuvées' for their wines.

After the base wines have been blended they are bottled, and yeast and sugar are added for the second fermentation. It is then left to mature and gain complexity. This usually takes at least five years and sometimes even longer. Once it is judged ready, it is riddled (rotated until the bottles are neck-down so that sediment collects there) disgorged (the sediment is removed) and allowed to rest for a further six months before shipping.

Nyetimber has pioneered the reputation of the UK's ability to produce a sparkling wine that rivals Champagne and has helped strengthen the perception that English wine is really worth drinking. The Nyetimber vintages have won top awards and gold medals, beating the best France can offer in blind tasting tests on both sides of the Channel.

Nyetimber currently produces two wines; a Blanc de Blancs (i.e. 100 per cent Chardonnay) and the Classic Cuvée made with a blend of the three grapes used in Champagne – Chardonnay, Pinot Noir and Pinot Meunier. The vineyard is not currently open to the public, but Nyetimber is available at good independent wine merchants throughout the UK. It is served at many high profile events, including the IOC dinner at Buckingham Palace which helped secure London's bid for the 2012 Olympics, and at top restaurants, including Gordon Ramsay, The Fat Duck, Oxo Tower, The Ritz and Rick Stein. Nyetimber can clearly give the Champenoise a run for their money.

Interesting fact: Nyetimber wine has been served at 10 Downing Street, Buckingham Palace and the House of Commons.

The Maldon Crystal Salt Company Ltd

What they make: sea salt
Founder: Thomas Elsey Bland
Founded: 1882
Based: Maldon, Essex

IN ESSEX, people have been producing salt from seawater for centuries; possibly since Saxon times and certainly since 1086, when the existence of 45 salt pans in the area is recorded in the *Domesday Book*. A popular legend suggests that the secret of salt making may have been discovered back when the Romans occupied Britain; a legion commander, Cassius Petox, was in the habit of easing his aching bones (brought about by our lovely British weather) by taking hot seawater baths. On one occasion the water was kept boiling for too long, and Cassius noticed that salt

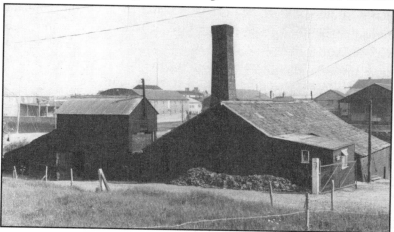

crystals had appeared at the bottom of the bath. He managed to pick them out and gave them to his fellow officers, who requested more – the first salt trade in Essex? Perhaps…

Maldon has always been recognised as an important salt-making centre; indeed, the Maldon Crystal Salt Company stands on the remains of what may have once been a medieval salt works. Maldon Crystal Salt Company was only used as a trade name for the first time in 1882 when Mr Thomas Elsey Bland, a wine merchant and Justice of the Peace, took over the existing salt company. It is currently run by the Osborne family, and has been since 1922.

Seawater for salt-making is usually taken from the spring tides, when the water is at its saltiest, and transferred to tanks in order to settle. After filtering, it's then drawn off as required to fill the salt pans. Despite the presence of twenty-first-century thermostatic controls, maintaining the correct temperature during evaporation is still a difficult task, requiring careful human attention to

sound and movement of the water and the speed of crystal formation. After evaporation, the salt crystals are collected by hand using traditional methods known as 'drawing the pans', before being dried and graded, also by hand.

Maldon salt is completely natural, unlike ordinary table salt, which is often highly processed. It has a cleaner, fresher taste than most salts, and a little goes a long way because it is so potent – good for those of us on low-salt diets. Humans need a measure of salt in their diet, and the salt composition of our tissues is pretty similar to that of seawater. This makes Maldon salt a quick and easy way of meeting some of our daily nutritional needs. Maldon Salt, much loved by celebrity chef Nigella Lawson, has been granted approved product status by the Organic Food Federation.

Interesting fact: The Maldon Crystal Salt Company is the smallest of the four salt-making companies in Britain, and the only one that still uses some of the traditions of Essex craftsmen to make its salt.

Tregothnan

What they make: tea (as well as essential oils, bouquets, wreaths and garlands from the flowers grown on-site, and charcoal and bespoke joinery)

Founders: the Boscawen family

Founded: the Boscawen family have owned Tregothnan estate since 1335, although they have only been growing tea since 1999

Based: Truro, Cornwall

Number of staff: 65

TODAY, AS on every other day, over 165 million cups of tea will be consumed in Britain. Of this, 96 per cent will come from tea bags made from crops grown in India, Africa and the Asian subcontinent. Our national drink, for which we are renowned around the world, wasn't actually made in Britain at all until a few years ago. A small British company based in Cornwall changed this.

During World War Two, when the UK feared supply routes might be cut off by the U-boats, commercial British tea growing was considered but never took off as the ground, climate and local knowledge were not deemed up to the task. The real 'English cup of tea' had to wait until the head gardener at the Tregothnan estate in Truro, Cornwall, took up the baton some fifty years later when he got the tea bug during his horticultural studies at the Royal Botanical Gardens in Edinburgh.

Tea comes from a type of Camellia bush, related to the ornamental Camellia that Tregothnan was also first to grow outside in the UK 200 years ago. With the belief that tea could be grown in the South West of England, Jonathan Jones set about planting the crop and, within six years, the first cups of tea were coming out of England. By learning the trade, selecting the most suitable types of tea bush and utilising an excellent Cornish micro-climate that provides great growing conditions, Tregothnan now produce the finest and most British tea.

The history of this most quintessential of British companies in tea is short, but in that time they have gone from being laughed at by the tea trade for entertaining the very idea of growing tea in England to being highly respected tea connoisseurs. A stiff upper lip and a 'never say never' attitude could hardly have been more appropriate.

To make tea at Tregothnan the tea leaves are hand-picked freshly at dawn; the top two leaves and a bud are taken to the withering racks where they are gently withered to encourage softening. After this, the leaves are rolled between two surfaces, traditionally by hand. Next, to promote oxidation or fermentation, the tea is spread on a surface at a controlled temperature, with the liquid already present in the cells interacting to change the colour from green to brown. Finally, they dry the leaves to two per cent moisture, and all this is done without the use of chemicals, with processes that have been sustainable for four millenia. Only 36 hours after the leaves have been plucked from their plants, the tea is ready for drinking.

Tregothnan now sells five varieties of tea through an increasing number of outlets as word of mouth and continued media interest in their locally-grown tea increases the popularity of their brand. In future they hope to make the Tregothnan Estate the romantic home of tea by building an International Tea Centre complete with tea rooms, galleries, gardens and a complete history of tea.

Interesting fact: 40 per cent of the daily intake of liquid in the UK comes from tea.

Walkers Shortbread Ltd

What they make: shortbread, cakes and biscuits
Founder: Joseph Walker
Founded: 1898
Based: Aberlour-on-Spey, Scotland
Number of staff: 1,000–1,300 (in peak production times)

INDEPENDENT, FAMILY-RUN businesses are titchy, right?
Maybe not – consider Walkers Shortbread Ltd.

The 21-year-old Joseph Walker opened his village bakery in
1898 with a loan of £50. His business quickly became successful
as shooting parties from the local estates dropped in to sample his
delicious produce, and soon he was able to move to a larger shop

and invest in a horse and cart. He ran the bakery until the 1930s when his two sons, James and Joseph, took over.

The 1930s was a time of expansion – James and Joseph introduced a selection of cakes and confectionery to their product list, and also purchased the company's first delivery van, enabling them to sell further afield. World War Two reduced their scope – both sons were kept busy as members of the Home Guard, and rationing also affected the company's profits – but the business kept going. Both during and after the war it maintained its high standards; by the 1950s, many biscuit manufacturers were using margarine instead of butter to make their products, but Walkers refused to cut corners in this way – a gamble that evidently paid off, for by 1961 they had 14 vans and shops in Grantown and Elgin.

By the end of the 1960s the bakery had expanded to supply the whole of the Speyside area and demand for shortbread had greatly increased; Walkers was now supplying it to many top London stores, including Harrods, its first private label account.

By the early 1970s the company was forced to expand; in 1970 they employed 100 people and were exporting to 60 countries, still using Joseph Walker's original recipe. A factory was built on the edge of the village and today it contains five units. Further expansion since means that Walkers now has 250,000 square foot of production space and 140,000 square foot of warehouse space. It is now the largest family-run biscuit manufacturer in the UK – currently run by the original Joseph Walker's grandchildren – its products are the fastest selling biscuits in the world wide duty-free market, and it represents 50 per cent of the UK shortbread market. Many of the people who worked for the company in the 1970s are still with them now, and whole families often work for Walkers. And their new products are all road-tested in Aberlour's village shop.

In 2002 the Queen awarded Walkers the royal warrant for supplying oatcakes to her, and the company also makes a range of organic biscuits under the Duchy Originals Ltd brand, the company established by Prince Charles that promotes sustainable farming and raises money for the Prince's Trust. Walkers is the only food manufacturing company to have won the Queen's Award for Export Achievement three times, the biggest honour given to British exporters. It has also won the Food From Britain Award three times, which is open to the entire UK food industry.

Walkers have managed to combine a booming business with a respect for tradition, and produce delicious, traditionally made shortbread, biscuits and oatcakes on a larger scale, exporting British delicacies to a worldwide audience.

Interesting fact: Walkers are the only major shortbread and biscuit manufacturer in Britain that is still independent and run by the family of the original founder.

Wilkin & Sons

What they make: Tiptree Jams
Founder: A. C. Wilkin
Founded: 1885
Based: Tiptree, Essex
Number of staff: 11, plus hundreds of fruit pickers

CHILDHOOD MEMORIES often reserve a nostalgic place for jam making: kneeling on a stool watching the bubbling mixture, the smell of simmering fruit intoxicating in its sweetness. The Wilkins, from their home in Essex, took this passion one step further and in 1885 sold their first jar of preserve from the family farm in the sleepy village of Tiptree, whose name the jam bears today.

The Wilkin family tree dates back to 1729 when John Wilkin and Mary Goodman met and married. When Charles Wilkin was born in 1799 the French Revolution was reaching its gory climax on the streets of Paris and while Queen Victoria was reigning sovereign, Charles Wilkin was busy growing fruit on the Tiptree farm. Against a backdrop of world upheaval, the quiet Essex

countryside was getting on with the Wilkin family tradition of farming and fruit growing. Today, Peter Wilkin, a direct descendant, is at the helm of the Tiptree business.

The founder of the company, A. C. Wilkin,

was a busy man; he not only fought for the development of the 'Crab and Winkle' railway from Kelvedon to Tollesbury, but also helped set up an old age relief scheme in Tiptree. By the time state pensions were introduced in 1911, £4,600 had been distributed to the workers. The company also built accommodation for its staff; in 1910 it owned 29 cottages in and around the village. Many of its workers live on the estate today. The Wilkin Provident Trust was established in 1917, with the motto, 'By their fruits shall ye know them', and a share of the profits was allocated to it for the benefit of the Tiptree employees. The company also set up its own minimum pension scheme, and gave out service awards to its most loyal workers.

Caravanners, locals and students make up the fruit-pickers who gather the fruit each year; during the strawberry season, up to 1,000 pickers can be found collecting fruit in the fields. Many of the caravanners stay on the Wilkin farm during the fruit-picking season, and some return every year to help pick – the company awards them a long service award after 21 years.

Picking is at its peak during strawberry season and continues until October, when the plums and quinces are brought in. By the end of October, the only fruit left to harvest is the medlar, an unusual fruit that looks like a cross between a rose hip and an apple; medlar jelly is a red preserve that goes well with pork and, traditionally, medlars are left out until after the first frosts, or Bonfire Night. Then the harvesting is over for the year, although Tiptree continues to work with Mediterranean fruits such as apricots and peaches.

Every fruit you can think of and a few more besides are grown at the Wilkin farm. Strawberries, raspberries, mulberries, loganberries, damsons, plums, crab apple, greengage and quince are all grown in natural conditions, picked by hand and turned, on site, into a wonderful array of preserves, jellies, curds and savoury delights that make waking up and having breakfast a culinary treat.

Interesting fact: The Persians were preserving fruit to supply vitamins all year around over two thousand years ago.

Tools and Machines

Ampair

What they make:	micro wind and water turbines
Founder:	Hugh Mereweather
Founded:	pre-1973
Based:	Warfield, Berkshire
Number of staff:	10

SINCE 1973, Ampair wind turbines and water turbines have been powering many thousands of remote homes, yachts, scientific and commercial locations worldwide. The company was formed by Hugh Mereweather, a former test pilot whose amazing life deserves a mention here. He was one of the first British test pilots who pioneered VSTOL (vertical short take-off and landing) through the experimental P.1127 which eventually led to the Harrier Jump Jet, an instantly recognisable and awesome piece of British engineering. He subsequently received an OBE and awards for bravery due to his unnerving ability to crash-land planes rather than eject, thus preserving the aircraft for engineers to check for faults.

Mereweather retired from test flying in 1970 and became an art dealer with a particular interest in maritime art. Around this time he purchased a 38-ft Camper Nicholson yawl, *Blue Idyll*,

which he sailed, with little previous experience, to Grenada. This is where his love affair with the ocean and the Ampair story begins, for he built the initial wind charger for his own yacht.

Since then, Ampair have been working in the renewable energy field. They have been designing and manufacturing wind driven generators that can survive in the severest of environments on land or sea, from Alaska to the Antarctic to the Sahara. Their British engineering is highly sought after and they are the first port of call for anyone wishing to lower their energy bills, or power batteries and engines where no power grid is accessible. With the continued push for reduced carbon footprint and the news that Prince Charles is now running a carbon neutral household, the clamour for integrated renewable energy in the home is becoming more popular and, with the likes of Ampair, more feasible. Solar power requires constant

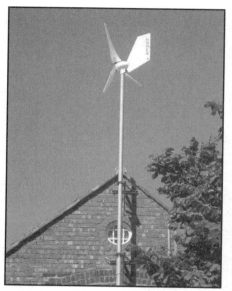

sun, a need which cannot always be met, so wind, as part of an integrated approach, is the ideal element to exploit.

In the beginning, Ampair was making wind turbines with a power output of 25 W; since those early days output has now reached 600 W and this increased power means the turbines are increasingly used in grant-supported low carbon housing developments. Where huge wind turbine fields can be unfriendly to the surroundings, micro-generation offers a viable solution. If you have a grid connected house, office or factory, then once the micro-wind turbine has been purchased you have energy for free. So there are good reasons to install micro-generation wherever you are.

Interesting fact: Ampair have a sideline in manufacturing alternators for vintage British motorcycles.

Bramah

What they make: locks and safes
Founder: Joseph Bramah
Founded: 1784
Based: Marylebone, London and Romford, Essex
Number of staff: 23

THE IDEA of a lock is to keep people out and possessions within. Simple really. Or so you would think. But alas, as long as inventors and manufacturers have been designing and constructing them, the criminal mind has been picking and breaking them, or at least, when it comes to Bramah locks and safes, trying.

Such is the esteem, history and reputation of Bramah locks that their history can be traced through classical literature. Charles Dickens wrote of them in *The Pickwick Papers*, as did George Bernard Shaw in *An Unsocial Socialist*. But it is the thrillers of Frederick Forsyth and Peter Wright where their complex and original locking mechanisms are most accurately described and their quality praised.

'Jagger demonstrated how to attack various locks. Bramah locks, used for diamond safes, were by far the most difficult. The pins moved horizontally through the lock and it is impossible to pick.' *Spycatcher,* Peter Wright

Yale and Chubb locks may be more recognisable and popular throughout the world but it is the British engineering of Bramah locks and safes that are widely regarded as the best, the hardest to pick and the most secure. In fact, the Bramah design came some fifty years ahead of the Chubb design and seventy ahead of the Yale lock, making it the first multi-functional locking mechanism of world repute.

The history of the company dates back to 1784 when Joseph Bramah designed a round lock mechanism operated by a tubular key. Three years later the lock was awarded a patent but not before

Joseph demonstrated its complexity and security by putting it in his shop window and offering a 200 guinea reward for anyone who could open it. Such was the tenacity and brilliance of the design that it wasn't until 1851 at the Great Exhibition in London that A. C.

Hobbs finally claimed the prize after spending 52 hours over 16 days picking the lock. And he was a master locksmith.

In 1901 they were awarded a royal warrant by King George V and started making locks for the king, who naturally had some quite valuable commodities to be kept under lock and key.

Today Bramah has expanded into burglar alarm systems and general locksmithing. Their locks are still in demand and used in all manner of environments and surroundings – from a

World Heritage site to an explosives store, from a jewellery shop in Knightsbridge to a butcher's in Carlisle.

Interesting fact: Joseph Bramah was a leading inventor during the industrial revolution, patenting over 18 new ideas, including a lock, a new valve for the water closet (toilet), the hydraulic pump, a fountain pen, and a fire engine. Bramah also introduced a hand pump for use at the bar, to prevent the loss of beer that occurred when barmen had to go downstairs to pour a new jug.

Burgon and Ball

What they make: gardening tools and
sheep-shearing equipment
Founders: Charles Burgon and James Ball
Founded: 1730
Based: Sheffield, Yorkshire
Number of staff: 40

ASK THE man in the street what he thinks of when he pictures Britain and you'll probably get a range of answers, but it's not unlikely that somewhere in there will be mentioned sheep and gardening. Burgon and Ball are Britain's oldest manufacturer of gardening tools and Britain's only manufacturer of sheep shears.

The company of Burgon and Ball began life as a factory overlooking the Don Valley in the industrial heartland of Sheffield

that manufactured knives, scissors and shears. It flourished and by 1873 had moved to new premises at Malin Bridge, in the west of the city, where it remains today. This site had been cleared after the disastrous 1864 Great Sheffield Flood, when the Dale Dyke Reservoir burst. The company built the La Plata works here; the buildings border the River Loxley, which supplied energy to the factory for much of the twentieth century.

In the 1880s the Ball family were bought out of the company, but the name remained the same. By now business was booming; sales of patented design sheep shears exploded, and in one year 300,000 pairs were sold. The company was also getting into the international market, selling to North and South America, Australia and New Zealand, and the West Indies; and they were developing a sheep shearing machine, the Daisy

Shearing Machine, which rocked the farming world when it was released in the 1890s. It was a massive success until it was replaced by the Dreadnought in 1912.

Sheep are an integral part of our landscape. But who'd have thought that to this day Britain supply sheep shears to the Australians?

We are also a nation of gardeners. By the start of the twentieth century, the company were manufacturing an extensive range of gardening tools, and by 1920, production of garden shears had overtaken that of sheep shears. A 1922 catalogue shows that Burgon and Ball were even then stocking 96 different types of hoe. Their garden business has continued to flourish and today the company has a worldwide reputation for high-quality, durable and innovative garden tools – exporting to over forty countries.

All Burgon and Ball shears are handmade. A team of 'benders' work on manipulating and shaping the handle and blades of a sheep or garden shear – it takes two years to train to be a bender, and requires a high degree of skill. Because of this, long service and reliable tools are a key feature of the bender's job; some of the company's employees have worked there for over fifty years, and some of the tools they use are that old as well!

Burgon and Ball take a variety of steps to ensure that all their tools are long-lasting and reliable. For instance, they use special high-carbon Sheffield steel instead of cheaper mild steel to produce a sharper, long-lasting blade. They heat the blade at precise temperatures for an exact length of time in order to guarantee a particular level of hardness as measured by the Rockwell scale – this is the determining factor in how long the blade will stay sharp. Burgon and Ball are also the only shears company to double hollow grind the blades of their shears to give the finest edge – a process with the patent number 297 (pretty low, so the process is clearly an old-established practice).

Some of the more unusual items that Burgon and Ball has manufactured in its history include bicycle wheels and tyres and even cars – 15 La Plata cars were produced in the early 1900s. Burgon and Ball are still the largest manufacturer of sheep shears in the world and their export business is thriving – professional farmers demand the highest standards from their tools. The methods of production and the design of shears have not changed much over the last hundred years, but if it ain't broke…

Burgon and Ball pride themselves on not succumbing to the throwaway culture of the twenty-first century, proudly creating tools that will last for years and taking a great British tradition further into the future. Farming and gardening are both ways of celebrating the environment we live in, and whatever the future holds, Burgon and Ball will be there to allow us to continue that celebration.

Interesting fact: On 10 October 1891, Jack Howe sheared 321 sheep in seven hours 40 minutes at Alice Downs, Queensland; in 1901, Chris Lewis sheared 3,543 sheep with only one shear! Both were using Burgon and Ball equipment.

Colpac

What they make:	printed paperboard packaging and food service disposables
Founder:	Frank Coleman
Founded:	1937
Based:	Flitwick, Bedfordshire

PACKAGING. YOU might assume there's no way that it can be good for the environment; all that rubbish generated just by people unwrapping their sandwiches... However, Colpac would prove you wrong. Their paperboard is produced from renewable resources – forests which are maintained and used economically – and the finished product simply decomposes under the influence of the elements. Even the windows on the sandwich packets are made from PLA cornstarch material – that is, plastic made from the renewable resource cornstarch, rather than oil.

Commercial cardboard packaging was first made in England in 1817, by Sir Malcolm Thornhill, and by 1900 products were already being shipped in corrugated paper cartons rather than wooden boxes. Some thirty years later, Colpac was founded by Frank Coleman, a lay preacher based in Luton. Its initial main output was stitched boxes, which were much in demand from the Luton hat trade. Frank traded in straw board from the Netherlands;

in 1948 he sold the small business to Martin Goldman, who had come out of the army, having spent four years in a POW camp in Austria during World War Two.

Cardboard packaging was becoming widespread with the popularity of flaked cereals (the first company to use cardboard to make their cereal cartons was Kelloggs) and the boom in cardboard use quickly spread to the other areas of the food industry; among other advantages, you could print things on it. Colpac went from strength to strength. It moved from Luton to Flitwick in the 1970s, and gradually expanded its output from stitched and rigid boxes to cartons, sandwich packs, tortilla and bagel containers.

Colpac produces a wide range of environmentally friendly packaging, and supplies packaging machinery that allows users to create compostable, biodegradable packs, containers and seals. It exports to over thirty countries, but is still a family-run business; its current managing director, Neil Goldman, is the son of Martin Goldman.

Colpac handles the entire process of creation itself, from product design and construction through to manufacturing and distribution. In 2001, the company set up its own laser die cutting facility – most packaging companies still outsource this work. 2004 saw the creation of Colpac Creative and Colpac Commercial,  studios to spread Colpac's design and printing skills. Colpac is one of the few packaging companies in the UK that offers such a wide range of techniques under one roof, thus using twenty-first-century technology to embrace current environmental concerns.

Colpac fulfils our need for packaging materials with creativity, practicality and flair. The company has won both a Mid-Beds Innovation Award and an East of England 'Smart Award', and has worked with or is approved by customers as prestigious as Sainsbury's and the Tate. It is a shining example of a company that can adapt to the times and is helping us, in the most natural way, to save our planet.

Interesting fact: Colpac specialise in designing and manufacturing biodegradable packaging for the food service industry, including a range of moulded plates and bowls that, given the right conditions, can biodegrade in weeks.

Corin Group Plc

What they make: reconstructive orthopaedic devices
Founder: Peter Gibson
Founded: 1985
Based: Cirencester, Gloucestershire
Number of staff: 290

CORIN GROUP – named after Corinium, the Roman name for Cirencester – had its identity clear from the start: a British company, providing high quality implants at competitive prices with outstanding service. Hip resurfacing, a process designed to help patients with an active lifestyle who have severe osteoarthritis of the hips, was pioneered and developed by Corin Group. Said to be the most important advance in orthopaedic surgery of the last two decades, this technology allows its users to maintain

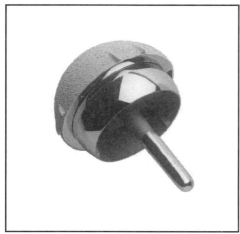

their high activity levels – something that just didn't happen with conventional hip replacement.

The first knee joint replacement was developed in 1947, but was a basic hinge joint, with little attempt made to mimic the design of a real knee. In the late 1960s the Gunston knee came along, the first replacement knee joint to have a metal-to-plastic articulation. All modern designs involved a compromise between allowing freedom of movement and making sure the components fit together well. Corin's Rotaglide Mobile Bearing Knee has the longest clinical history of any knee replacement of its type which

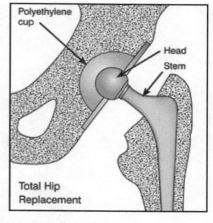

permits both rotation and front-to-back movement.

Something that dramatically affects an implant's longevity is the production of polyethylene particles created by wear and tear, as the body may perceive these as a threat, put up its defences and cause the loosening of the prosthetic to occur faster. Currently it is not possible to eliminate polyethylene from replacement knee joints completely, but the better the pieces of the joint fit together, the fewer particles are produced. As younger patients may have an activity level 20–30 times higher than that of elderly patients, there is more wear and tear leading to more particles being produced. However, Corin's Rotaglide Knee has a survival rate of 98 per cent after eight to nine years.

Hip replacements operate on the same principles and once again, Corin are leading the way. In the late 1980s, they teamed up with British surgeons and scientists to design a metal-on-metal hip replacement implant for the younger patient. This has a number of advantages over conventional total hip replacement: it involves less removal of bone; Corin were able to eliminate polyethylene in the bearing of the implant, which also means it will last longer; and the bearing is more stable and eliminates risk of dislocation.

115

The twenty-first century has seen Corin successfully floated on the London Stock Exchange, and it has also acquired Alphanorm, a German orthopaedics company. Let's hope the positive trend continues, because its work is vital.

Interesting fact: Army instructor Steve Boswell is the first man in the world with two hip replacements to have completed the North Pole Marathon, a 26.2-mile course run on four-metre thick drifting Arctic ice floes. Who supplied the replacements? Corin, of course.

Greenaway Marine

What they make: equipment for video cameras to enable them to be used underwater
Founder: Stephen Greenaway
Founded: 1972
Based: Swindon, Wiltshire
Number of staff: 5

GREENAWAY MARINE are a comparatively young company compared to some in this book, but a prime example of British spirit and enterprise. The company have actually been making their own products only for the last 15 years, after they decided that the products they were importing from other countries were too fragile, had too many problems when used underwater, or just didn't help produce an image of good enough quality.

You may or may not know that using a still camera to take photographs underwater while diving is probably not going to yield images of high quality without a lot of very expensive equipment and practice. This is why Greenaway Marine suggest that using a video camera is better — it will give you far better results with much less effort, plus you can also record your undersea adventures continuously, rather than waiting for

photo opportunities. To allow you to do this, Greenaway can provide Seapro underwater camera housings for any video camera in the world, and it doesn't end there. Most housings have flat ports, which reduce the angle of view underwater, but Greenaway Marine's unique Optolite Port is curved, with wide angle capabilities. This means that the images will be sharp and clear whether they were taken underwater, above water, or when you were bobbing up and down on the surface.

Greenaway's housings are used by professionals in the photography, television and film industries; they're very robust (because taking a camera diving can mean subjecting it to a lot of pressure if you decide to dive deep) and the company are happy to build housings for specific cameras.

Greenaway also manufacture colour correction filters; for use underwater in 'blue' water, that is, water containing coral reefs, requires an orangey-red filter; 'green' water, or British, Atlantic and Mediterranean seas, requires a mauve one. The deeper you go, the more colour, especially reds, oranges and yellows, are lost to the natural filtering properties of the water, and a colour correction filter removes the 'cast' from the water and enhances natural colours, allowing you to record the true colours of what you are filming. Then there are water detectors to warn you if your camera is getting wet, video lights, and a wide range of other equipment to allow people to produce amazing images of the wonders below the ocean's surface. Greenaway Marine's Seapro housings were recently rated the best in both performance and value in a survey of leading manufacturers of housings, so they know what they're talking about.

By buying Greenaway Marine's British-made products, you are reducing your carbon footprint, and by using them to record the beauties of the deep you are making people clearly aware of some of the wonders our earth can offer – and why we need to save it.

Interesting fact: You can take a video camera down to a depth of 85 metres underwater when using a Greenaway Marine Seapro housing.

Hiatt and Co. Ltd

What they make:	handcuffs and police batons
Founder:	Mr Hiat
Founded:	1780
Based:	Birmingham, West Midlands
Number of staff:	17

BRITISH PEOPLE come in all shapes, sizes and inclinations, and it's a sad truth that as long as there have been people on these shores, there have been criminals of one kind or another – and where there are crooks, there have to be ways of dealing with them. In 1780, Mr Hiat – the company name only later changed to the 'Hiatt' spelling – opened a factory at 26 Masshouse Lane specialising in 'prisoners' handcuffs, felons' leg irons, gang chains'... Unfortunately his business also supplied collars for black slaves. Could such a company change with the times? It seems to have done.

During the nineteenth century, the War Office, the Foreign Office and the Admiralty were among Hiatt's high-profile customers, and it also exported products to the USA, where New York's police force was a steady client. The business remained at Masshouse Lane for over 150 years; metalworkers made components in wrought cast iron, which were then hand-assembled by skilled handcuff fitters. The first Trade Directory record of the company is in 1832, although the Hiat family may no longer have had any connection with it. The first British police force obtained its first pair of cuffs from Hiatt soon after its formation in 1829, and

London's Metropolitan Police still get their equipment from the company today.

In the second half of the nineteenth century Hiatt and Co. began making animal restraints, including nose rings for bulls and pigs. However, focus switched back to human restraints when World War One began – handcuff makers had to work from seven in the morning until nine at night to meet demands. Even after the war, demand remained high – during the General Strike of 1926, policemen queued all the way down Masshouse Lane to get hold of whistles, cuffs and truncheons. World War Two yielded a burgeoning market for whistles, rattles and handbells for sounding warnings and all-clears; but in April 1941 the entire area around Masshouse Lane was destroyed by incendiary bombs. Luckily, some quick action by a young fire-watcher and a hosepipe meant that the machine shop, containing the most valuable tools, was saved, and the following day the company moved into part of Fan Disc Ltd's premises in Northwood Street. It remained there until 1947, when it built a new factory in the suburb of Great Barr; it is still based there today.

Hiatt tapped into another massive market when it became the first manufacturer in England to make a plastic cable clip for holding cables to walls or door frames. Electrics and television sales were booming, and this sideline was so successful, eventually producing 4,000,000 clips per week, that Hiatt were able to sell it as a separate business in 1978.

The company currently represents 90 per cent of the home market, selling to prisons, police forces, customs, airlines and security organisations, including those protecting monarchs and world leaders all over the globe. It was actually sold to a US buyer in 2006, but all its products are still made in Birmingham, with no sign that this will change.

Hiatt's range of handcuffs is wider than that of any other manufacturer, and meets or exceeds all quality standards dictated by the United States National Institute of Justice. They also make the world's only folding rigid handcuff and a modern range of 'snap-on' cuffs which can be put on quickly – handy in scary situations. All their cuffs also have 22 locking positions to accommodate any size wrist.

When Mr Hiat started his business, prisoners' collars and shackles were fastened with rivets; today more sophisticated locking systems are used, but Hiatt and Co. have kept pace with technological change and are still performing a valuable service.

Interesting fact: Hiatt supplies handcuffs to virtually every police force in the world.

JCB

What they make:	(in the UK) backhoe loaders, telescopic handlers, tracked and wheeled excavators, mini excavators, skid steer loaders, rough terrain forklifts, telescopic lift trucks, wheeled loading shovels, articulated dump trucks and Fastrac tractors.
Founder:	Joseph Cyril Bamford
Founded:	1945
Based:	Rocester, Staffordshire
Number of staff:	5,000+

CHANCES ARE that if you are sitting in the confines of a building that has been constructed in the last 30 years, somewhere along the line JCB will have been involved in the construction. JCB is now the third largest construction machine manufacturer in the world and with strongholds in India, Europe, and the Middle East and growing ventures in China and Russia, the future for this British giant is assured. But it wasn't always like this.

JCB's is the story of a man with a dream in the shed at the bottom of his garden... well, almost. In 1945 Joseph Cyril Bamford set up in his lock-up garage in Uttoxeter,

Staffordshire. With nothing but a 50 shilling welder and some surplus war material he built a simple trailer.

In the proceeding 62 years JCB has become a billion pound, global business manufacturing over 55,000 machines in 2006 alone, becoming the third largest construction equipment manufacturer in the world and producing some 279 different machines in their unmistakable bright yellow. Although not all their manufacturing is done in Britain, they do have 10 manufacturing plants in Britain, their headquarters is still near Uttoxeter, in Rocester, and the son of Joseph Bamford, Sir Anthony Bamford, is at the helm as chairman of the company.

At the heart of JCB's success, from an engineering perspective at least, are hydraulics, and it was this simple theory (that force applied at one point can be transferred to another via an uncompressible liquid, in this case, oil) that pushed the designers and engineers at JCB. This potential for hydraulic lifting was first utilised in 1948 with possibly the world's first hydraulic trailer. This was followed up in 1953 by the first backhoe loader (the archetypal 'digger' shape of JCB) and the rapid rise to building site necessity began.

Since those early days JCB has won more than fifty major awards for engineering excellence, export, design and for its care for the environment. The latter can be seen with the environmentally conscious JCB Dieselmax engine which went into production in November 2004. Operating at Tier II emissions levels the engine is cleaner and kinder to the environment. More than 50,000 Dieselmax engines have since been produced.

JCB is not only doing its part in reducing CO_2 emissions but is also one of the first to act in any humanitarian relief effort. In 2005 JCB joined a global relief effort in earthquake-torn India and Pakistan and donated over £500,000 worth of machines. Their tracked excavators, designed for arduous quarrying and demolition work, were used by the Pakistan Army to clear roads and collapsed buildings. The company also donated over £1 million of machines to the Tsunami disaster where JCB machines were deployed in southern India, Sri Lanka and Indonesia to help clean up the devastation and try to restore a sense of normality.

JCB pride themselves on being a company that never stands still, constantly seeking new horizons. Determined to help their customers to do a better job, JCB is a global operation that is run as a family business.

Interesting fact: In August 2006 the JCB Dieselmax car, fitted with two high performance diesel engines, set a new world record for a diesel powered car of 350.092 mph on the Bonneville Salt Flats in Utah, USA.

Kirkpatrick Ltd

What they make: malleable iron products
Founder: William Kirkpatrick
Founded: 1855
Based: Walsall, West Midlands
Number of staff: 108

MALLEABLE IRON is a type of cast iron that is treated with a heating process known as annealing. Whilst in contact with haematite ore, the iron is heated for up to 100 hours at around 1,000°C. At Kirkpatrick Ltd they know the advantages that malleable iron, with its greater flexibility and greater tensile strength, has when making handles, latches and hinges.

William Kirkpatrick, Esq., J. P., founded Kirkpatrick in Walsall in 1855. The business was carried on for many years in his name and under his direction. After his death in 1887 his son, Vincent Kirkpatrick, took over the business which was incorporated in 1901 as a limited company. Many long-serving employees were given a shareholding at this time and this tradition of employee shareholders continues to this day. Whilst the Kirkpatrick family still retain a shareholding they no longer control the company.

Unlike other ranges of architectural ironmongery, Kirkpatrick products (with a few exceptions) are made from whiteheart malleable iron which is durable and well suited for use on doors and windows, for example. Together with traditional manufacturing methods which have not changed, in essence, for more than 150 years this means that Kirkpatrick products have a style and authenticity which other more modern products lack.

Whilst retaining their traditions, Kirkpatrick also strive to modernise to keep up with their competitors and offer superior products to their customers. To do this they have invested in

an electric melting facility, which allows the company to produce a more consistent quality of iron. At the same time, it permits Kirkpatrick to meet the environment standards required by current UK legislation. Meanwhile, unlike cheaper imports, Kirkpatrick Ltd products don't have to travel halfway across the world in order to supply their British customers.

Kirkpatrick Ltd has over 2,500 products in their two ranges of black ironmongery, which are the antique ironwork collection and the general ironwork collection. The antique ironwork line has authentic textured patterns, which adds old English charm to doors, windows and furnishings, whereas the general ironwork line has smooth surfaces and a more gothic look. Both ranges comprise similar items designed in several different styles. If you need a reliable bolt, doorknocker, gate latch or boot scraper that's made in Britain, ask for Kirkpatrick.

Interesting fact: The company logo of a hand holding a dagger, and the company motto 'I mak siccar', relate to the family name Kirkpatrick and its involvement in an important event in Scottish history. John Comyn, who had designs to become the King of Scotland, had a quarrel with Robert the Bruce. Bruce stabbed Comyn but, rushing away, shouted to his escorts, 'I doubt I have slain Comyn'. Roger Kirkpatrick replied, 'I mak siccar' – 'I'll make certain' – and, upon finding Comyn still alive, proceeded to stab him through the heart. Subsequently, Robert the Bruce was crowned King of Scotland.

Robert Sorby

What they make:	woodworking hand tools
Founder:	Robert Sorby
Founded:	1828
Based:	Sheffield, South Yorkshire
Number of staff:	35

ROBERT SORBY can trace its tool-making heritage back to 1624, though the earliest history is sketchy at best. The first mention of the contemporary company is in 1828 when it was registered in Union Street, Sheffield, as a manufacturer of edge tools, saws, scythes and hay knives. As a result of the invention of crucible steel in 1742, Sheffield edge-tool and saw manufacturers were way ahead of their competitors by the mid-nineteenth century. Robert Sorby is the only one to survive to the modern day, making them the oldest manufacturer of hand tools in Sheffield.

Robert Sorby ran the business until his death in 1857, and was responsible for expanding the company so it remained competitive, as well as widening their product range to include axes, augurs, joiner tools, hooks and sheep shears. The company also began merchanting and manufacturing crucible steel.

Like many other companies, Robert Sorby ventured overseas to find a market for their goods. Marketing their products in Australia and New Zealand led them to name their factory back in England the Kangaroo Works. The Kangaroo would remain a registered trademark of Robert Sorby until the mid-1980s.

The company remained in the Sorby family until 1904 when Thomas Heathcote Sorby died. Before his death, he acquired John Wilson Marsden, a company that produced edge tools but were better known for supplying ice skates to the royal family. In the years that Robert Sorby produced skates, they always exceeded the sales of the edge tools.

Even though the business was out of Sorby hands it continued to flourish and acquired another edge tools manufacturing business, James Howarth and Sons of Bath Street in 1922. One year later, Robert Sorby and Sons itself was bought by Hattersley and Davidson, a Sheffield engineering company. Recognising the importance of the company, Hattersley and Davidson allowed it to retain its identity and it remained a separate trading entity, although relocated to Hattersley and Davidson's production site on Chesterfield Road in 1934.

In the 1960s, the business began to place more emphasis on its woodturning range and so successful was this move that it allowed the business to de-merge from its parent company in 1985. At the same time they sold off their gardening, agricultural and ice skate interests, shortened the company name to Robert Sorby and moved its factory to a new location.

Today Robert Sorby is the world's premier manufacturer of specialist woodworking tools – woodcarving and woodturning tools, woodworkers' chisels and lathe accessories – with dealers in Europe, North America, Australia and New Zealand and the UK. Its employees still use the traditional methods passed down from the early cutlery industry at the Sheffield factory. They say: 'Because it has our name on it we will stand by that product.'

Interesting fact: In 1624, by an act of Parliament, the Company of Cutlers was formed in Hallamshire, Sheffield, 'for the good order and government of the makers of knives, sickles, shears, scissors and other cutlery wares in Hallamshire'. The first master cutler was a Robert Soresby.

Smith Bros (Quinton) Ltd

What they make: wooden packaging, including tea chests
Founders: Cliff and Ran Smith
Founded: 1927
Based: Tipton, West Midlands
Number of staff: 35

BROTHERS CLIFF and Ran Smith set up their business at a time when work was difficult to come by due to the recession gripping the world. The two decided to try and make a go of things on their own rather than looking for an employer, and established their business in Quinton, Birmingham, in 1927. The company started

off making 'foster mothers', that is, timber incubation units for chickens, as well as sheds and garages, porches and verandas, and anything else wooden that their customers required.

However, such construction requires nails and screws, paint and putty, and glass, and so the brothers set up Smith Bros (Quinton) Ltd Ironmongers. The business continued to grow until World War Two, by which time five of the six Smith brothers were now involved in it. During the war, production of timber buildings was suspended in favour of that of ammunition boxes – Smith Bros produced thousands of these to do their bit for the war effort.

After the war the company returned to its old trade, but wood was in short supply. The company managed to buy some 'Canadian timber invasion barges' from the Ministry of Defence which were moored on the Thames at Hammersmith. Despite the difficulties of dismantling them – the first one took several days and a gang of men to take apart – they yielded a good quantity of useful timber.

In the early 1950s, Cliff Smith was contacted by an acquaintance from the Austin Motor Company and asked if Smith Bros would be interested in providing export packing cases for what would later become the Rover Group. The brothers decided to accept the opportunity, and became the sole supplier of packing cases to the Rover Group, as well as the major or only supplier to most large and volume users of export packing cases.

In 1960, the company set up a factory in Scotland to provide export packing cases for the Bathgate Truck Manufacturing Facility

and Rootes at Lynwood; the latter became known eventually as Peugeot.

In 1998 the company set up a new division, SBQ Flexible, which produced woven plastic sacks and flexible packaging. It soon became very successful, supplying both the local Midlands area and all of the UK. In 2003, however, it was sold, to allow the company to focus on its specialist carpentry and woodworking skills.

In 2004 the company moved to a modern production facility in Tipton where new storage facilities and an automated pallet production unit could be installed. The third generation of the original Smith family are still involved in the company.

Smith Bros now sources timber from Britain, Ireland, Scandinavia, Russia and the Baltic states, and wherever possible it gets its wood from sustainable, carefully managed forests. Environmentally, it's in a good position to start with – wood has the lowest energy consumption and the lowest CO_2 emission of any packaging material, and using wood products actually encourages forestry to expand – if demand for wood drops, the usual effect is that land is deforested and used for something that will make more of a profit. This, plus the fact that the Smith Bros products often provide a non-disposable alternative to conventional plastic packaging or storage boxes, means if you want to save the planet, you could do a lot worse than look them up.

Interesting fact: For every cubic metre of wood used instead of other building material, 0.8 tonnes less CO_2 is emitted into the atmosphere.

Valeport Limited

What they make:	surveying and monitoring equipment
Founder:	Jim Stephens
Founded:	1969
Based:	Totnes, Devon
Number of staff:	42

VALEPORT CAME from meagre beginnings, producing a small range of river monitoring equipment. They are now the UK's leading manufacturer of hydrographic and oceanographic instrumentation – an extensive range of surveying and monitoring equipment for the oceanographic, coastal, estuarine and hydrographic communities. They are represented by agents in 40 countries around the world.

So how does a company so small become the UK's leading manufacturer in their area of business? Well, developing sought-after technology was the key to Valeport's success. The team at Valeport developed products such as CTDs and tide gauges, and they instantly became top sellers. The CTD is perhaps the most commonly used tool in an oceanographer's armoury, providing detailed profile and time series data on conductivity, temperature and pressure, and the calculated values of salinity, density and sound velocity. The exploration of the North Sea during the 1980s made the 600 series CTD a popular choice, and their tide gauges started finding their way into many ports and harbours around the world.

During the late 1990s, they saw another opportunity to fill a gap in the market. They embarked upon a new phase of development, coming up with innovative wave recorders and velocity instruments. Their Model 730 directional wave recorder provided customers working on coastal projects with the opportunity to gather data where traditional methods continued to fail. This was a huge step forward for coastal research around the world.

Valeport's continuous product development has kept them ahead of the game, and the competition, for decades. Their products cover every aspect of surveying and monitoring – one of the latest innovations being a range of mini-sensors and profilers that provide their customers with extremely accurate results using digital circuitry and up-to-the-minute technology.

From its base in Totnes, Devon, Valeport carries out a remarkable amount of research, development, design, manufacturing and testing. Their facilities include a full mechanical workshop, electronics test equipment and environmental chambers. Plus, of course, their access to the River Dart, its estuary and the open sea are essential for testing and developing their products. Manufacturing processes include original mechanical design, firmware and software design, machining of metals and plastics, in-house circuit and wiring loom assembly, cable terminations, product assembly and testing and calibration.

Valeport promise their customers a service that is second to none – a crucial part of every successful business.

Interesting fact: Valeport is at the forefront of technology and has an international customer base so diverse it includes environment agencies, universities, ports, harbours, the military and research institutes.

135

Walters and Walters

What they make:	industrial crayons
Founder:	W. L. Bird
Founded:	1894
Based:	Royston, Hertfordshire
Number of staff:	4

ESTABLISHED IN 1894 by W. L. Bird, who purchased the plant and machinery from C. J. Price, shellac recover and sealing wax manufacturers, the business of Walters and Walters was first carried out at Bagleys Lane, Fulham, then moved to Newington Green in North London when the property was acquired by the local council for street improvements. In 1984 the company moved from there to Royston in Hertfordshire.

The current managing director's grandfather and father worked for a competitor and saw an opportunity to buy Walters and Walters just after World War Two. She started to work at the company right after college, as did her daughter, which makes her the fourth generation of the family to work at Walters and Walters.

The company manufactures and distributes all types of industrial marking products and still manufacture industrial crayons at their factory in Royston. The manufacturing process is very much the same as it has always been, although the introduction of health and safety procedures and EU regulations has meant that the crayons themselves have had to change significantly over the years.

If you need a crayon to mark any kind of surface, Walters and Walters can provide it. They are economical, clean and easy to use and they are all non-toxic. Each type is specifically formulated to produce a clear bright mark on the given surface including timber, metal, rubber, glass, stone and masonry as well as everyday marking of paper and card. Road-markers remain among the most popular – large rectangular sticks of wax that will mark all road surfaces.

Over the years, the company has diversified into many different areas but industrial marking remains the core of their business. Walters find that they supply their products into almost every kind of industry. Road workers, metal workers, power stations, paper factories, engineers and rubber moulders, to name a few, all use Walters products.

They supply to customers all over the UK and since the introduction of the Internet, they now send their products as far afield as the Arctic Circle and Australia.

Interesting fact: The company has had patents awarded for Woods Patent Sealing Wax Burner; Inventions 'Ivynoid' Gelatine Bottle Capping Adhesive and 'Ivoline', a water soluble adhesive for cloth not affected by a hot iron.

Sports and Music

Bowers and Wilkins

What they make: speakers
Founders: John Bowers and Peter Hayward
Founded: 1966
Based: Worthing, West Sussex
Number of staff: 306 in the UK

JOHN BOWERS spent World War Two as a special operations executive, focusing on radio transmissions and maintaining contact with allied resistance operatives in occupied Europe. He was also very fond of classical music and disappointed with the quality of the existing loudspeaker technology. After the war, he opened a hi-fi store with business partner Roy Wilkins and began building his own loudspeaker designs at the back of the shop; the start of a quest to create the perfect loudspeaker. His custom-designed speakers quickly gained a reputation for high-quality sound reproduction, and fate took a hand when an elderly lady, Miss Knight, who had

been impressed both by Bowers' knowledge of classical music and by the speakers he made her, died and left him £10,000 to develop a business. Bowers and his friend Peter Hayward agreed to live modestly and put any profits they made back into the business, and in 1966, B&W Electronics Ltd was formed. The company produced its first commercial loudspeaker, the P1, later that year, and in 1968 they launched their first domestic monitors, the DM1 and DM3.

John Bowers' close links with recording engineers helped him to see what made loudspeakers successful. In 1970, the company produced the DM70 loudspeaker, which had a massive impact on loudspeaker design – its clear sound was a revelation. Then in 1979 the 801 loudspeaker was launched, and soon became the reference speaker in recording studios worldwide – including Abbey Road and Decca Records. The 801 used superior drive units, kept in separate chambers, and ushered in the modern era of loudspeaker design.

Bowers used the profits from the success of the 801 to fund the Steyning Research Establishment, a research facility for his engineers in West Sussex. Created in 1981 and often referred to as 'The University of Sound' by journalists, it gave the engineers access to a wide range of modelling, testing and design tools and is now universally regarded as being at the forefront of loudspeaker research.

John Bowers died in 1986, but his company's success continued. Abbey Road installed the company's Matrix 801 models in its studios – the relationship between the two bodies continues today. In 1993 the company launched the Nautilus, also described as 'the best loudspeaker money can buy'; it was the company's first loudspeaker without straight sides, and

changed the face of Bowers and Wilkins speakers. 1997 saw the introduction of the Nautilus 800 Series which confirmed B&W as the market leader of high-end loudspeakers. This range was up-graded in 2005 and featured many new technologies including diamond dome tweeters (most speakers up until then had used aluminium) which greatly improve reproduction of high notes, due to their rigidity.

In 2006 the company celebrated its fortieth anniversary. Today it continues to use the latest technology and discover new innovations to improve the sound quality of its products. For instance, when constructing the sensitive drive units, humans carry out the tasks requiring analysis and a careful eye, such as fitting dust caps and placing the units in cabinets; while robots perform tasks like gluing, where precision is vitally important and a speck of glue in the wrong place can affect performance later. The glue is also mixed with UV dye, so that once the unit has been constructed, UV light can be used to detect any seeping or smearing. Just a few examples of how the company is moving with the times in attempting to fulfil John Bowers' dream of creating the perfect speaker.

Interesting fact: The cones of Bowers and Wilkins loudspeakers are made of Kevlar, the same material used in bullet-proof vests.

Drakes Pride

What they make:	bowls and bowling accessories
Founder:	Darlington's
Founded:	traced back to Darlington's
Based:	Liverpool, Merseyside
Number of staff:	19

POPULAR IN Britain since the thirteenth century and now an international sport being played in over thirty-five countries, bowls is 'a game of delicate skill, the object being to get bowls as close as possible to the target'. It is surprising, therefore, that a company heavily involved with both the manufacturing of bowls and playing the game has only been around since the 1960s.

Drakes Pride was a registered trademark before it was a company. It originates from another Liverpool-based company, Darlington's,

which was believed to have used it throughout their history. The business itself is far more recent, dating to the 1960s when Darlington's was acquisitioned by E. A. Clare & Son Ltd. Already manufacturers of other sporting goods, E. A. Clare & Son decided to expand into lawn bowls.

During this period there was a redesigning of bowls, with the wood (*Lignum vitae*) that was conventionally used in the manufacture of bowls disappearing. It was replaced with the manmade Phenolic Thermoset, and with this and modern machinery, Drakes Pride relaunched in 1982, producing bowls that had greater accuracy and consistency than the more traditionally made ones. This improvement was a result of Drakes Pride being the first company to use computer-controlled lathes, which allowed for the bowls to be made to a more accurate specification.

Drakes Pride bowls are frequently used in professional competitions worldwide and the company are licensed manufacturers for several governing bodies including the Lawn Green and Crown Green. Drakes are even the licensed jacks manufacturer for the British Crown Green Bowls Association. By stamping and testing all makes of bowls, Drakes Pride are able to remain in contact with their consumers, listen to their comments and adapt their bowls accordingly. As Drakes Pride puts it, they 'are committed to helping promote the sport through all levels from the "grass roots" amateur to the professional game'.

Today, Drakes Pride creates bowls for the amateur as well as the professional bowler and produces a variety of sets, from ones that are designed for speed to mini-bowls designed for young children. They even design bowls for an international level, listening to players in different countries and adapting the bowls to allow for the different ground conditions.

As well as bowls, Drakes Pride also makes accessories to further enhance the game, including bags, measures, polishes and hand warmers. They even have their own line of bowling clothes and shoes. To further expand their market, Drakes has also ventured into indoor games, with a range of skittle sets and table and carpet bowls kits, bringing the game inside and to a new client-base.

Interesting fact: On 15 July 1588 Sir Francis Drake refused to leave for battle until he had completed his game of bowls on Plymouth Hoe.

Gordon-Smith Guitars

What they make:	electric guitars
Founders:	Gordon Whittam and John Smith
Founded:	early 1970s
Based:	Partington, Greater Manchester
Number of staff:	3 self-employed luthiers

FOUNDED OVER 25 years ago by Gordon Whittam and John Smith, Gordon-Smith Guitars is one of the longest running contemporary guitar-makers in Britain with sales in the UK, Europe, Canada, USA, New Zealand and Japan. It is not surprising therefore that the magazine *Guitarmaker* has said that 'Gordon-Smith Guitars are to England as Gibson Guitars are to the USA.' High praise indeed.

Gordon moved on to other projects in 1981, but luthier John Smith has continued to run the business out of his workshop in Partington, priding himself on crafting guitars that are attractive, solidly built, well designed and 'extremely playable', but still reasonably priced for working musicians.

Over the years, the business has produced over 9,000 guitars, and is run by John, his wife Linda and their friend Chris. Each has their own section of the production line: John designs the guitar, shapes it from a block of wood and later sprays it, Linda preps the surface before and between the finishing coats and winds and assembles the pick-ups, and Chris levels and buffs the final finish. Chris also assembles the parts, strings the guitar, fits the nuts and fine tunes the product so it is ready for sale. With John being an excellent

luthier, he is quoted to have said, 'Our products are like the Zippo lighter, there's nothing to go wrong so it doesn't.'

Unlike other companies that prefer to use hard maple to build the bodies, John prefers the softer Tulipwood or even yellow pine in order to achieve the sounds he wants from the guitars. Everything except the tuners are made to John's design specifications, which have been crafted to achieve the best from each and every guitar produced. With unique hand-assembled pickups and fully adjustable bridge and beautiful tremolo, you really do get a uniquely British instrument.

One of the things that stand out with Gordon-Smith Guitars are their optional solid maple necks that are void of a rear-mounted truss-rod and therefore a 'skunk stripe'. This is due to John's discovery of a way to drill a curved hole into the maple to insert the truss-rod. After three years of perfecting this method, John

is unsurprisingly secretive about how he achieved this feat.

Along with the guarantee of a great guitar, Gordon-Smith also offers reasonable prices and doesn't charge extra for requirements such as left-handed guitars or single or double-cutaway. Whilst they don't design guitars to customer specifications, as far as possible they will add the customer's own guitar parts, offering discounted prices for those wanting to do it that way.

Gordon-Smith say: 'It is true to say that the guitars have been the workhorses of many British pro and semi-pro bands over the past 25 years and quite a few in Europe as well... If we can be of any assistance, please don't hesitate to call, write, fax, e-mail, carrier pigeon or whatever turns you on. For now, take care, be happy and enjoy yer music.'

Interesting fact: Gordon-Smith guitars are used by professional musicians such as Spike Edney who has worked with Queen, Duran Duran and the Rolling Stones.

Grays of Cambridge

What they make: sporting equipment
Founder: Henry John Gray
Founded: 1855
Based: Robertsbridge, East Sussex
Number of staff: 100

GRAYS OF Cambridge has been responsible for some of the best sporting equipment around for the past 150 years and the equipment they manufacture has been used by top sporting personalities in the fields of cricket, rugby, hockey and racket sports. The company has managed to build up a generous list of reputable brand names, primarily through acquisition and growth.

Henry John Gray, known to most as 'Harry', founded the business. At a young age he was employed at the rackets courts of the University Arms Tavern in Cambridge, and it was here that he learned the trade of making rackets and balls. Harry also excelled as a rackets player, becoming World Champion in 1863. He founded H. J. Gray and Sons in 1855, and the company started selling racket balls and stringing rackets. Growing rapidly, the company soon expanded into cricket bats.

Harry retired in 1896 and the company passed into the hands of his son, Horace. By then, H. J. Gray and Sons had grown to include a shop at 8 Rose Crescent, a factory in Searle Street, a London office and even a golf course in Grantchester. Under Horace the business continued to expand, with major innovations helping to boost the company's popularity. One of these was the Masterpiece Lawn Tennis racket which, unlike other rackets of the period, had laminations instead of a solid frame. This helped to improve both the shape of the racket and its performance.

Being based in Cambridge meant that Grays had a steady stream of customers in the form of university students and this helped them to become endorsed by players, such as England's Davis Cup captain, Max Woosnam. This increase in business prompted a move to bigger premises to cope with the growing manufacture of their products.

The outbreak of World War One led to the factory assisting with the war effort, producing tent poles, picket posts, stretchers,

tables and mallets. Douglas Gray, one of Horace's sons, was sent to fight in the war and won the *Croix de Guerre* for acts of heroism. On his return home in 1919 he helped his father to re-establish Grays, and it soon became a founding member of the British Sports Manufacturer's Association. Grays also extended their old factory and opened another in Ireland in association with local timber merchant Harry Russell.

By the 1930s, Grays had begun to acquire other sporting manufacturers, such as Nash and Co., and was winning endorsements from top sports personalities like Copper and Milford in tennis. Unfortunately, Douglas Gray died during this period of profit for the company, but his wife, Alison Rhone Gray, succeeded him in running the business.

Production was interrupted again by World War Two, with the factories helping by manufacturing tent poles, instrument panels for the Mosquito aircraft, barrage balloons and electrical parts. As a result of the war, the Concentration of Industries Act meant that Grays was appointed a nucleus firm and acquired ten other sporting firms.

Throughout this period Alison Gray worked to ensure that Grays was a brand seen at the highest levels and helped to maintain Grays' competitive edge by expanding their ranges. The company continued to thrive when her sons took control and the 1960s and 1970s saw Grays becoming a market leader in squash and hockey, again making acquisitions to bolster the success of the business.

The 1980s saw competition from imports, which led to Grays restructuring and the focus of the company shifted from rackets (which for a time was licensed to a third party) to hockey and cricket, though their businesses in Australia and Pakistan continued to prosper. In England, Grays was forced to sell off sites they had gained during the 1970s as the head office was moved to Robertsbridge in East Sussex.

Today, the Grays brands are expanding both here and abroad, with a merger with Gilbert Rugby in 2002 leading to Grays dominating the

world of rugby balls with the Gilbert brand. Cricket products are also booming for the firm with stars such as Mohammed Yousuf, Matthew Hayden and Alistair Cook breaking records with Gray-Nicolls bats such as the revolutionary Fusion – the first with a carbon handle. In hockey Grays lead the way with around fifty per cent of international players choosing Grays sticks in the 2006 world cup. In netball the Gilbert ball has been chosen for the 2007 world championships and in rugby league the Steeden ball is the ball of choice for all major matches – worldwide. Not forgetting their beginnings, Grays continue to handcraft real tennis rackets in Cambridge to this very day.

Interesting fact: In the Rugby World Cup 2003 final, Johnny Wilkinson delivered the winning drop kick with a ball made by Gilbert, a company acquired by Grays in 2002.

Harrod UK

What they make: sports and gardening equipment
Founder: Ron Harrod
Founded: 1954
Based: Lowestoft, Suffolk

RON HARROD set up his business over fifty years ago, with no business plan and no dreams of success, creating garden netting out of old herring nets. Little did he realise that within a few years, he would be running a thriving sports equipment business. Now Harrod UK manufactures every type of goal or net the sports world desires, from basketball posts to archery nets, rugby posts to cricket cages, hockey goals to high jump stands, while Harrod Horticultural, formed in 2000, can supply you with plant

supports, greenhouse staging, fruit and vegetable cages, and in fact anything you need to make your garden grow better (their catalogue, originally 16 pages long, is now over 100).

The company's philosophy of 'setting the standard' and 'leading the field' is pretty obvious when you think about who's been buying their products. Sports fans might be impressed to know that the games and matches you've been watching at the Premier League clubs, Wembley and the Manchester Commonwealth Games have all used goals and nets made by Harrod UK. You're not likely to see any shoddy workmanship at these world-class venues. Meanwhile, on the horticultural side, Harrod Horticultural provides equipment to some of the Royal Horticultural Society's most prestigious gardens.

Ron Harrod's belief in quality and safety has certainly helped him score when it comes to his success. To avoid serious accidents that can be caused by inadequate design or installation, Harrod dedicated his business to producing the crème de la crème of goal posts and nets. Harrod UK is now not only known as the UK's leading goal post manufacturer, it even plays a part in setting the safety standards for the UK as a representative in the CEN (Comitè de Europèan Normalisation). And gardeners need not worry either; the company rigorously tests most of its products in its kitchen garden, which has been running for two years, and customer focus groups all over the country are asked to provide input on new designs.

Moreover, Mr Harrod has kept his work ethic very much in the 'noughties'. Environmentally friendly Harrod says, 'Times are changing rapidly and we are also investing heavily in caring for the environment; the well-being of future generations is very much at the heart of company policy and decision-making.' Putting his money where his mouth is, he plans to have a 250 kW wind turbine installed, aimed to provide the business with its very own renewable energy source. Harrod Horticultural's credentials are no less impressive; its ethos is one of organic growing, and this has inspired it to widen its range from steel cages and nets to biological pest control, composting and garden ecology.

Clearly, Ron Harrod has come a long way since the days of herring nets. He admits 'every day is a challenge in business' – this thoroughly modern man seems to be rising to the challenge like a true champion.

Interesting fact: Harrod UK have made goals and nets for Wembley Stadium, Millenium Stadium, and England's World Cup training venue in Germany.

155

ITSA Goal

What they make:	mini-soccer uPVC goals-in-a-bag, full range of aluminium steel and uPVC goalposts for all age groups
Founder:	John Wilson
Founded:	1992
Based:	Sheffield, South Yorkshire
Number of staff:	10

AT THE age of ten, in 1959, John Wilson made a small 12 foot by six foot wooden goal with Woolworths pea netting to enable himself and his friends to play football in the summer holidays. Only full size goals and full size pitches were available for children to play in at that time and without nets. Fifteen years later, no development had taken place by the Football Association or makers of sports equipment, so out came the wood and pea netting again to make goals for his son.

With this in mind, John Wilson started the company ITSA Goal to manufacture a uPVC version of the goal he used as a boy. The new goals were smaller, lightweight and safer. Combined with proportionally smaller playing areas, mini-soccer allowed more touches of the ball in a game, closer contact and therefore the chance to develop and improve skills. This in turn encouraged more children to play and made it easier for girls to be introduced to the sport. With a special patented net fixing, John Wilson's new goal was designed to pack away in a carry bag.

Initially, however, it was scorned by retail sports distributors and school suppliers. As John had borrowed £50,000 to develop the idea, things weren't looking good. The Halifax Building Society helped by allowing a holiday period on a mortgage repayment – without this the company's future would have been doubtful.

It was as the Football Association were getting a hammering in the press about football development in England and lowering skills at grass roots level that ITSA Goal approached them with the mini-soccer concept. The FA took the new mini-soccer goal and tested it for three months, putting it up and down every day – after which they approved the product. During this test period ITSA Goal put together a Coca-Cola branded promotional pitch in red bags that held everything needed for children to set up a pitch anywhere, anytime. Enclosed were two goals, nets, bibs, corner poles with flags and pitch markers. Coca-Cola purchased bulk orders which were then sold on. The scheme was a win–win situation for all concerned: ITSA Goal attained large orders for their new product, Coca-Cola attained free branding at a targeted audience and the FA got good press for doing something about developing the game. This promotion continued for 11 years and enabled the company to survive and grow.

The original goal-in-a-bag concept has since been imitated in the UK and the Far East many times, but the company pride themselves on the quality of their designs and the customer satisfaction this brings. John Wilson believes in building lighter goals for children for ultimate safety. ITSA Goal has improved on the 'nuts-and-bolts' goalposts already on the market by welding their posts together and using an innovative, patented lockable system, which reduces the possibility of collapse through loss of parts, vandalism or carelessness. Perhaps partly for that reason, some of the biggest names in football including Gary Lineker choose their goals above others for their children, with Ray Stubbs saying 'Every school should have sets of goals like this.'

ITSA Goal create products at reasonable prices that are built to last, not to contribute to landfill sites in a few years. Many of the very first uPVC goals supplied two decades ago to clubs and schools are still in use. This is a company that loves the game and wants to communicate that love to a new generation.

Interesting fact: ITSA Goal have registered more goal-post designs and patents than any other UK goal manufacturer.

James Purdey and Sons

What they make: guns and rifles
Founder: James Purdey
Founded: 1814
Based: Mayfair and Hammersmith, London
Number of staff: 62

JAMES PURDEY completed his gunmaking apprenticeship in 1805, after which he worked for Joseph Manton, then London's top gun-maker, before starting his own business in 1814. In 1826 he took over Manton's premises on Oxford Street; the business would remain there until his son, also called James, built new premises, comprising a factory, showrooms and offices, in Mayfair in 1882. Over this period there were major technological changes taking place in the world of guns; the muzzle loading flintlocks of the 1820s had evolved to become breech loading hammerless ejectors. James the Younger was able to remain at the forefront of all this change; indeed, he took out several patents for gun-related innovations during his lifetime, many of which were taken up by other gun-makers, and are still being used today.

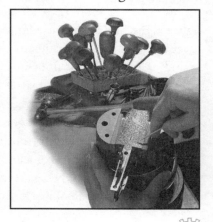

The Purdey factory moved to new premises in Paddington in 1900, and remained there

until 1975 when their buildings were acquired for redevelopment, propelling a relocation to Hammersmith. The factory is still there today, producing between 70 and 80 bespoke guns and rifles every year. The company still employs and trains skilled craftsmen to make its guns, while also investing in the latest digital (CNC) technology. This has significantly improved the quality of the component parts, which can now be manufactured to an accuracy of within one thousandth of an inch, and has also enabled Purdey craftsmen, who continue to use skills acquired and handed down over two centuries, to improve their productivity.

In 1946, the Purdey family sold the business to the Beaumont family, who owned it until 1994 – when it was acquired by the Richemont Group. However, at the Group's request, Richard Purdey, who is directly descended from the first James Purdey and is part of the sixth generation of the family, became chairman of the company in 1995 until his retirement in 2007, when he was succeeded by Nigel Beaumont, formerly managing director, a Purdey trained gun-maker, and a cousin of Richard Beaumont, the company's previous owner.

Purdey use walnut for the stocks for their guns; it is strong, lightweight, and beautifully figured. Walnut also does not crack as it ages. In the past the company experimented with other woods, including maple, but walnut was found to be the best choice – for instance, maple becomes brittle with age. Purdey use Turkish walnut wood, taken from where the root of the tree joins the trunk. When ordering new guns customers are able to choose their wood from a variety of different stock blanks.

All the component parts of a Purdey gun or rifle are manufactured in the company's own CNC machine shop, after which the craftsmen, using traditional gunmaking skills, hand shape them to build each gun or rifle individually. On arrival in the finishing shop, the gun's mechanical function is regulated: this is vital for absolute reliability, and has to be built in. Cam and sear firing points are adjusted for the correct sequence of operation for trigger pulls, striking, opening, ejecting and closing, all the time with total safety and reliability in mind. Once the gun is regulated it is thoroughly field tested before delivery.

Purdey still trains new gun-makers under its own apprentice system – they begin their training at the age of 16 in one of seven gunmaking trades – barrel making, action filing, lock and trigger making, ejector making, stocking, engraving or finishing. After five years apprentices qualify as craftsmen (or craftswomen) when they are permitted to stamp their initials on the particular parts of a gun that they create.

No two Purdeys are the same, though guns ordered as pairs come very close. Each new gun made to order takes between 18 and 24 months to deliver. When ordering, customers are advised on the specification of their new guns in accordance with their particular shooting needs, such as pheasant, grouse, quail, duck or upland game. All Purdey guns are made in the company's fully integrated factory in Hammersmith, West London under the personal supervision of Nigel Beaumont, who says: 'When we finish a new Purdey gun, our aim is not only to make it beautiful, but to make it work beautifully, for a hundred years and beyond'. That is the Purdey tradition.

Interesting fact: Queen Victoria bought a pair of Purdey pistols in 1838 – as a gift for the Imam of Muscat.

John Newbery Ltd

What they make: cricket bats
Founder: John Newbery
Founded: 1981
Based: Hove, East Sussex
Number of staff: 6 full-time and several part-time

PICTURE THE scene: a Sunday afternoon, the sun is shining and the air is still save for the occasional crack of leather on willow. A low ripple of applause and excited chatter bathe the cricket ground as the scoreboard leisurely ticks over. Newbery is part of this most romantic of sports, handcrafting cricket bats for all players of the game from their home at the county cricket ground in East Sussex.

A more appropriate home there is not. But Newbery products are also the result of detailed research and a combination of traditional skills and modern thinking to meet the demands of today's competitive game.

Newbery choose the finest willow for every cricket bat they make, usually from the South East of England where every year they plant, maintain and fell an increasing number of willow trees, ensuring that the trees and the bats will be around for future generations to enjoy.

Newbery can trace its heritage back to the early 1900s, when the Newbery family first made cricket bats in Robertsbridge. John Newbery's father, Len, was a bat-maker and partner of Nicolls Bats (later to become Gray-Nicolls, another famous cricket bat manufacturer) who had made bats since the time of W. G. Grace. Len's skills were handed down to his only son John, who founded Newbery in 1981. His reputation as a master bat-maker and his innovative designs became well known. Sadly, John Newbery died in 1989, but his senior craftsman Tim Keeley is the current managing director of Newbery, and using the same skills to produce cricket bats as John did.

The skill of handcrafting cricket bats is an art form that is learnt over many years. Newbery cricket bats begin life as carefully selected willow trees. Each cleft is individually assessed and, if accepted, will have been judged favourably for its weight, grain and performance, the three most important factors when judging the quality of a cricket bat. Common to all bats is the treble spring handle, and care is given to the binding with strong Irish linen thread, which tunes the flex of the handle.

163

The primitive bat is given its individual character by the craftsman who cuts and shaves the willow to a weight and balance specified only by his experience. It is his job to make the best out of every single cleft. As the shaping and balancing of each Newbery bat is done by hand and eye, every cricket bat has an original and individual feel and performance to it. Traditional tools such as the drawknife, spokeshave and block-plane are used to shape the blade before it is pressed, sanded and polished.

A cricket bat is a precious instrument that contributes to the player's game. Newbery's philosophy is that quality, performance and style come first.

Interesting fact: Dominic Cork, Murray Goodwin, Carl Hopkinson and James Kirtley have all used Newbery bats.

Leon Paul

What they make: fencing equipment
Founder: Leon Paul
Founded: 1925
Based: Hendon, London
Number of staff: 30

IT'S A good sign when a company is not just involved in manufacturing products for a sport but also participates competitively in it. Leon Paul is a fourth-generation family business that prides itself on being a British fencing manufacturer, supplying not just the UK but also the United States.

In 1905, a French officer from Perpignan visited England as part of his grand tour of Europe after his departure from the

French army. With his fencing diploma, Leon Paul became the assistant of Lucien Morel, though with the start of World War One he was forced to put his fencing career on hold to work as an interpreter. When he returned to London in 1920, he married Anna, a Lithuanian woman, who helped his fencing business by taking care of the clothing whilst Leon assembled the weapons and

masks. At the same time he was teaching fencing at Eton College, the BBC and the Imperial College.

Moving to a larger house in 1928 allowed Leon Paul to open the Salle Paul on its ground floor, a fencing club of about twenty members, which included professionals such as doctors and lawyers. The house was big enough for the basement to be a men's changing room and shower room, the first floor the shop and women's changing room and the upper floor the living quarters. Leon Paul also set up a forge opposite the house, making it the perfect place for a fencing business.

The outbreak of World War Two signalled a turbulent time for Leon Paul as their premises in Monmouth Street were badly damaged, prompting a move to a smaller site down the road which could only hold the shop. Rationing limited materials for fencing equipment, causing Anna to find more economical fabrics to make clothes from; their son Rene, when he was on leave, would mend the broken foils and blades with solder and wire. The Salle Paul stayed open by finding premises wherever it could.

In the 1960s, the ownership of the company passed into the hands of Rene and their youngest son Raymond, with Rene taking care of the production and tailoring while Raymond secured the commercial success of Leon Paul. This partnership benefited the company for over twenty-five years, and during this period, Rene's son Barry established a foundry for making blades in Neasden, where it would remain until the company transferred its interests to King's Cross in 1996. In the same year, Raymond

retired, leaving the running of the company to his son Steven and Rene's son Barry. Steven left to pursue a career in another aspect of fencing, leaving Barry to run the business with his wife Joan and their two sons Ben and Alex. Today they make over 800 fencing-related products, including foils, masks and clothing and their annual turnover has doubled in the past five years.

Nearly all members of the Paul family are keen competitive fencers and collectively have participated in 20 Olympic Games, 30 World Championships and have won 25 national titles.

Interesting fact: Leon Paul has its own fencing team that consists of some of the finest UK and international players.

Marshall Amplification

What they make:	guitar amplifiers and speaker cabinets
Founder:	Dr James (Jim) Marshall OBE
Founded:	1962
Based:	Bletchley, Buckinghamshire
Number of staff:	220

IF THEY were good enough for Jimi Hendrix, they are good enough for me. That the Marshall amplifier was partly responsible for the sound of perhaps the most talented and influential guitarist of our time is testament to the excellence of these British-made amplifiers. When 'The Star Spangled Banner' rang out over the diminishing crowds of Woodstock in 1969 and Jimi Hendrix signalled the death knell for the 1960s and a generation with that immortal tone, he did so through a Marshall amp.

The story started almost a decade earlier when Jim Marshall had a small music shop in Hanwell, London, mostly selling drums and accessories. The drummers tended to come in with other members of the band and soon Jim was being asked if he could supply guitars. As a result, Jim expanded his range to include both guitars and amplifiers. Then, one day in 1962, a young local guitarist

called Pete Townshend walked into the shop and complained to Jim about the amplifier he was using and asked if anything could be done.

In response, Jim enlisted the help of Ken Bran (his engineer) and Dudley Craven, and they set about making the first Marshall amplifier.

The amplifier was built using locally sourced components where possible and after a few prototypes that didn't quite meet Jim's strict requirements, they produced the very first Marshall amplifier which can still be seen today in the Marshall museum at the factory and is referred to as Number 1.

Jim used KT66 valves which gave the amplifier what has become known as 'the Marshall tone' and it soon found favour with musicians in London. One such guitarist was Eric Clapton. When Clapton joined the Bluesbreakers he asked Jim to build a combo amplifier – the result was the Bluesbreaker, and its monumental sound can be heard on the legendary '*Beano*' album.

The progression of Marshall is inextricably linked to the bands and musicians of the 1960s. For example, when Pete Townshend and John Entwhistle of The Who approached Marshall looking for extra volume, the result was the now famous 100 watt valve amplifier and was also the birth of the renowned stack, now seen on nearly every stage throughout the world. It was Jim who, after building an eight by twelve cab for Pete, cut this cabinet in half and turned it into the now legendary stack, consisting of two four by twelve cabinets with an angled cabinet placed on top. The extra volume was received with great acclaim and caused a Spinal Tap-esque battle for more volume between the two men. Pete Townshend went back to Marshall, who doubled the number of output valves, utilised a larger power transformer and also added an extra output transformer. Basically, what this meant is that ears are still ringing. The design was updated and is now known as the SLP 100.

Not long after the first 100 watt was made, James Marshall Hendrix visited Britain. He plugged into Eric Clapton's Marshalls and was immediately hooked on them. As his drummer, Mitch Mitchell, had been taught to play the drums by Jim and had worked in the shop on a Saturday, Mitch took Jimmy to meet Jim Marshall. *Axis: Bold as Love* was released the following year.

With the supply of KT66 valves becoming difficult, Jim was forced into a valve change to the EL34 and this resulted in an even more distorted and aggressive sound. The EL34 is still the most common valve used in amplification today, although the KT66 has made a comeback more recently.

The 1970s saw massive innovation with the introduction of the first transistor heads and the Master Volume series in an attempt to control the brutal sound. During the 1980s and 1990s Marshall experienced stiff competition from across the Atlantic, but Marshall resolve was unflinching. The JCM2000 range, the JVM series and the smaller, more affordable, solid state amplifiers are all keeping Marshall at the very forefront. Their future is perhaps in the hands of the next Jimi Hendrix, still playing guitar licks in their bedroom through a British built Marshall amp and yet to be discovered.

Interesting fact: Queen, Guns 'n' Roses, The Who, Jimi Hendrix, Eric Clapton, Metallica and Nirvana have all used Marshall amps.

Peradon

What they make:	cues
Founder:	Leopold George Peradon
Founded:	1885
Based:	Liverpool, Merseyside
Number of staff:	12

YOU MIGHT be forgiven for thinking Peradon is a French company because of its name, but in fact it is named after its founder, Leopold George Peradon, the son of a skilled church furniture-maker that settled in England from France. Apart from the name, Peradon is British through and through.

In 1885, Leopold found a niche in the cue-making industry. Before Peradon, cues were imported unfinished from France

and then British craftsman would work them by hand to their completed state. Leopold, rather than buying into this business, decided to make his cues from scratch, working from his home in Linacre Road in Willesden. His wife would aid him by polishing and packing the finished cues, which he would then deliver by trap and pony. The benefit of self-delivering was that whilst dropping off his products, Peradon would get new orders directly from the London billiard traders. To get pointers on how to further his business, Leopold sent his two sons, Frederick George and Louis Fraser to internships in France, who then brought the knowledge they acquired back to benefit their father's business in England.

The original business manufactured plain ash cues, before expanding into one point, two point and four point hand-spliced cues. Years later they would also manufacture the four point machine-spliced cue that is still in use today.

It wasn't until the invention of the cue lathe in the early twentieth century that business really began to take off. Whereas before the average craftsman could produce up to ten to 12 cues per day, with the lathe it shot up to 140 and it wasn't long before demand meant that Peradon had to open a second factory, this one in Beauvais, France – although with the outbreak of World War One in 1914, additional output from the French factory was prevented from being shipped over to Britain.

It was in 1929–1930 that demand for billiard cues increased dramatically due to the opening of several thousand billiard

halls across Britain, and demand for small cues rose when under-sized billiard tables became popular in the household. Eager to increase sales further still, Frederick Peradon from the original Willesden factory

helped to expand into the export market, appealing to the wider audience by producing other equipment used in billiards, including balls, cloth, rubber etc. His son Bill Peradon helped in this venture and eventually took control of the company post-World War Two. During this period Peradon acquired three other cue-making businesses; Nidd's of Kentish Town, MacMorran's of Chalk Farm and Weilding's of Acton, making Peradon the only remaining cue manufacturer in the British Commonwealth.

In 1966, Peradon moved its factory to Andover in Hampshire where Charles Gage joined the company. When Bill Peradon's son decided that he would not succeed his father in running Peradon, Bill decided to amalgamate with E. L. Fletcher & Son Ltd in 1976.

Today, Peradon produces several ranges of cues, including the MacMorran American cues, which are hand-selected cue shafts, kiln dried and precision turned to a Pro-Taper, finished with a white fibre ferrule and 13 mm tip. Peradon also uses the Internet to their advantage by offering a bespoke service where the customer can design a cue to their own specifications.

Interesting fact: During World War One, Peradon produced sticks to be used for signalling flags. These were given to the Ministry of Munitions because wireless communication was not in use between military units.

173

Thurston

What they make:	billiard and snooker tables
Founder:	John Thurston
Founded:	1799
Based:	Liverpool, Merseyside
Number of staff:	68

'**THE NAME** of Thurston is synonymous with billiards history,' boasted a sales pamphlet for Thurston in 1949. Indeed, Thurston has been heavily involved with the game of billiards for centuries. The founder, John Thurston, learnt his trade at Gillows of Lancaster's London office, making furniture and billiard tables. In 1799, the Thurston furniture business was set up at Newcastle Street in The Strand, and probably also at Catherine Street. Thurston's subsequent move to Waterloo Billiard Works in Chelsea for manufacturing purposes indicated a shift in focus towards billiard tables and billiard room furniture. Having a factory by the Thames meant it was easy to receive the timber they required to be shipped to them.

The Thurston offices also had a match room where they held

billiards competitions, and this tradition continued when they were forced to relocate to Leicester Square in 1901. It was at this address where their match room was visited by members of the royal family and famous writers such as Arthur Conan Doyle and J. B. Priestley. The Leicester Square offices also had showrooms and, with Thurston contracting architects and artists to design tables for them, it was ideal. Thurston began to invest in overseas opportunities by opening an office in South Africa, with some of the annual general meetings for the entire company being held in Cape Town.

Severe bomb damage as a result of the Blitz in 1940 meant another relocation, this time to Cheyne Walk in Chelsea. Post World War Two, the company enjoyed success by adding snooker tables to their products, but it was a disruptive period for the business. In the second half of the twentieth century, the company moved several times, and its fortunes began ailing somewhat, prompting an acquisition by E. A. Clare & Son.

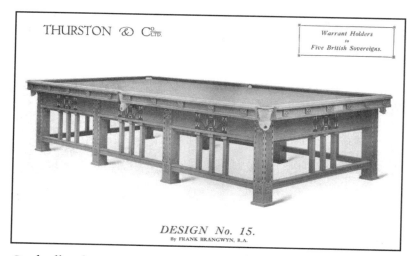

THURSTON & C°LTD.

Warrant Holders
to
Five British Sovereigns.

DESIGN No. 15.
By FRANK BRANGWYN, R.A.

Gradually, there was an increased demand for billiard and snooker tables in the UK, Hong Kong, Belgium and Holland, and eventually all manufacture of Thurston products moved to their factory in Liverpool. Today, Thurston has offices in Birmingham and Liverpool as well as its Edgware offices.

Since its founding, Thurston has become involved in every aspect of billiards and snooker equipment manufacture, but tables remain the staple of the company. Their tables have been given exhibition awards and been issued with royal warrants. The basic structure and specifications of the billiard and snooker table have the remained the same since 1892 when The Billiards Association selected the Thurston table as 'the standard'. It is even possible to trace some of the older individual Thurston tables and find out their exact histories due to the complete records Thurston keep dating back to 1886.

Interesting fact: The writer J. B. Priestley was so impressed by the Thurston match room in Leicester Square that he wrote an essay entitled 'At Thurston's', which was published in 1932.

For the Home

Aga

What they make: range cookers
Founded: the original Aga company was founded
in Sweden in 1922
Based: Ketley and Coalbrookdale, Shropshire

PEOPLE GET attached to their Aga. Really attached. Perhaps it has something to do with the continuous radiating warmth they emit or memories of cosy winter evenings huddled against the stove, tea in hand. Maybe the beautiful curves and lines, the reliability and the energy-saving attributes are reason for the attraction. Once thought of as traditional and gentrified, it is now cool to own an Aga and its popularity is soaring.

The original Aga was invented in 1922 by Dr Gustaf Dalén, a Nobel Prize winner for physics and a devoted husband. Blinded in an horrific accident, he used his time spent convalescing to realise his blueprint for the perfect cooker. He wanted to free his wife from the inefficient and sometimes dangerous stoves of the day, but never got to see the cooker that was to become a kitchen icon around the world.

He harnessed the principle of stored heat, a simple yet highly efficient way of regulating temperature that utilises the immense heat-storing capacity of iron. The heat is conducted under the hotplates and around the oven, which means it is always up to temperature and always ready to use. The same principle is used today. The design has been updated, more colours have been added to the range and, most importantly of all, the means by which it

is fuelled was updated some time ago. Initially only available as a solid-fuel range, it can now be powered by gas, oil or even a standard 13-amp electric plug.

The Aga itself is almost completely made from recycled products, the main constituent being scrap iron. Old car parts, pipes, gates and gutters are all recycled and used in the manufacturing process and when old cookers are finished with, they are simply recycled and used in a new generation. The cooking life of an Aga could be well over 100 years but the real lifetime could be many more. The stove you have at home could still be used in a thousand years.

In an increasingly environmentally conscious culture, Aga has embraced the zeitgeist. The company has unveiled the AIMS Aga, a fully programmable model, and a new generation of biofuel-ready models. Once these organic fuels become commercially available a slight modification to the Aga burner will result in the greenest of green cooking appliances.

Often imitated, the Aga is a unique piece of British engineering and manufacturing that has a place in the hearts of lovers of all things quintessentially British, not just here but all over the globe; there is even one on Bird Island off the north tip of South Georgia.

Interesting fact: Agas are still made by hand at an historic foundry in the Shropshire hills at the very birthplace of the industrial revolution. The area has been designated by the United Nations as an internationally important World Heritage Site.

Bradley Furniture

What they make: classic English furniture
Founders: Messrs Tyler, Sullivan and Adams
Founded: 1973
Based: Folkestone, Kent
Number of staff: 20+

WHEN YOU think of furnishing your home, what is better than classical style furniture that can fit in with either the traditional family home or the most modern of decors? For over thirty years Bradley furniture has provided the British public and the world with high-quality furniture that does exactly that in mahogany, yew and more recently oak. Their designs are based on furniture from that most elegant of centuries, the eighteenth, but every piece has been refined to adapt to a more modern lifestyle.

Whilst their furniture has adapted, so too have their manufacturing methods. In their founding year, 1973, they were a small business of skilled craftsmen; now, after over thirty years in the industry, they have grown into a factory that is able to better meet the demands of their clientele and now ship their furniture all over Britain and Europe. Yet still, every member of staff employed by the factory is a highly skilled craftsperson and the result is the gleaming furniture that the company is famous for. Bradley prides itself on its hand-finished style and each piece of furniture goes through 14 stages of polishing and hand finishing; including speciality finishes that help to bring

out the furniture's natural beauty, before it reaches their high standards. This is not restricted to the wood either, with Bradley taking equal measures of care in the furniture's brass castings and veneers.

Originally Bradley had one collection, the well-established and respected Classic Collection that includes furniture for the bedroom, dining room, living area and study, all available in either mahogany, mellow mahogany or yew veneers. The furniture is designed to complement any decor, with its natural patina emerging as the furniture ages to create harmony with its surroundings. Now the range, which has over 100 items of furniture, is joined by the Newington Collection, a selection of oak-veneered furniture that combines beauty with sturdy craftsmanship. And for those people who want something with a more personal touch, Bradley offers a bespoke service that allows their customers to order furniture to their own design and specifications. The recent interest in more traditional style furniture has led to Bradley increasing their independent customer base both in the UK and overseas.

Bradley and several other furniture companies have formed the Woodland Heritage, an environment-friendly charity which works upon the idea that forests, rather than being merely preserved, should be maintained and re-developed and pursues all aspects of this, from scientific research for conservation to 'plant-a-tree' days. The Woodland Heritage understands that trees are our only renewable resource and as such provide traditional furniture makers and foresters with the opportunity to give back to the environment they take their materials from.

Interesting fact: Bradley Furniture is a founding member of the Woodland Heritage Scheme, which seeks to improve the way trees are grown, maintained and harvested in Britain.

Burgess, Dorling & Leigh Ltd

What they make:	pottery
Founder:	William Leigh
Founded:	1862
Based:	Stoke-on-Trent, Staffordshire
Number of staff:	60

AT THE pottery of Burgess, Dorling and Leigh, the clay is from Devon and Cornwall, and nineteenth-century machinery is involved in its processing. The company is the only one in the world still producing transfer printware; that is, transferring patterns onto china using tissue paper and then re-glazing the finished product to 'seal' the patterns. Their designs combine Victorian skills with contemporary style.

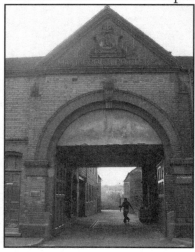

In 1851, a Mr Hulme and a Mr Booth set up a pottery in Burslem, Stoke-on-Trent. A decade later, William Leigh and Frederick Rathbone Burgess took over the running of the central pottery, changing the business name to Burgess & Leigh, and in 1889 the company moved to the newly built red-brick Middleport Pottery, adjoining the Trent and Mersey Canal. It was an innovative

place, the realisation of William
Leigh's vision to improve
efficiency and productivity
while also doing the utmost
to maintain good working
conditions.

William Leigh died in 1889,
Burgess in 1895, and the
business passed on to their sons,
Edmund Leigh and Richard
Burgess. When Richard died
in 1912, the Leigh family
became the sole owners of the
business. Edmund Leigh was
an indomitable campaigner for
pottery workers' rights (he even installed baths and basins for the
workers in the factory basement) and a key figure in the formation
of the British Pottery Manufacturers Federation. He was also a
Justice of the Peace, a Burslem town councillor, a Staffordshire
County Council member and a founding member of the National
Liberal Club.

By 1939 Burgess & Leigh Ltd employed approximately 500
people. Their designers were some of the leading lights of the
industry; for instance, Harold Bennett, a well-known water
colourist, created several designs for their tableware, and Charlotte
Rhead, a potter famous for her 'tubelined' designs, was employed
from 1926 to 1931. The company was by then exporting their
products to North America, Australia, New Zealand, South Africa
and Holland. A second wave of international trade arrived in 1965
when they began shipping to Western Europe and Scandinavia.
However, by the 1990s, although five generations of Leighs had
run the pottery, things were looking bleak. In June 1999, Burgess
& Leigh went into receivership just as the 55 employees were

about to begin their summer holiday, and the Middleport Pottery was threatened with demolition.

Enter Will and Rosemary Dorling, a couple who ran The China Box Company, a small ceramics mail order business in Hampshire, that counted Staffordshire pottery among its wares. They were very keen to support high-quality English pottery and 70 per cent of their sales came from Burgess and Leigh stock. Recognising the pottery as a 'hidden treasure of national importance' with its traditional moulds and patents, they were determined to save it rather than see the building gutted and turned into posh flats. Initially, they planned only to campaign, writing to heritage bodies such as the National Trust, but no one was able to offer financial support in time to beat the receiver's deadline. Will and Rosemary decided there was only one thing to do – buy the pottery themselves. With only £400 in the bank, they had to borrow from family and remortgage their house, but were able to put in a bid with minutes to spare – and won out.

Today the pottery is booming, while still using traditional English methods and raw materials. The raw materials are no longer delivered by canal, but clay is processed on the premises by the original steam-driven machinery. Cup handles are still attached by hand. As the *Daily Telegraph* wrote in 2000, 'Arnold Bennett would not have much difficulty in recognising the factory he featured in *Anna of the Five Towns*.'

After the company's lucky escape, it is hoped that its beautiful products will be around for years to come.

Interesting fact: Middleport Pottery, where the company's products are made, is the last operational Victorian pottery in England.

Charnwood

What they make: wood-burning and multi-fuel stoves
Founders: Alfred Wells with sons Alistair and John
Founded: 1972
Based: Newport, Isle of Wight
Number of staff: 150

FOR OVER thirty years, Charnwood, a family-based, privately owned company has provided stoves and boilers to customers all over Britain, making them the oldest manufacturer of wood-burning stoves in the country. Charnwood is part of the larger A. J. Wells & Sons Ltd, which was founded in 1972. Alfred Wells and his two sons set up a small engineering company in Niton on the Isle of Wight, keeping the company local in order to provide jobs and give back to their community. Today Charnwood exports its products to places throughout Europe, as well as to

Japan and South Africa, and employs over one hundred members of staff at their 50,000-square-foot factory, which has relocated to Newport. It is also run by the second and third generation of the Wells family, and at one point, up to seventeen members of the Wells family were working within the company.

Charnwood specialises in multi-fuel (solid fuels such as coal) and wood-burning stoves, though their products also include electrical and gas stoves and boilers, with several ranges catering to the needs of every customer. As far as possible they try to manufacture their products in-house in order to maintain full production control as well as ensuring that the stoves and boilers are made in as environmentally friendly a way as possible.

This idea of being 'green' extends past the manufacturing process to every aspect of the company, from choosing raw materials, recycling packaging and even how they transport their materials and products. As the website states, 'It is our view that it is environmentally unsustainable to transport heavy materials around the world, on the grounds of small savings, when the world's finest materials are available here in the UK.' With this in mind, Charnwood strives to buy British whenever possible.

When creating a stove or boiler, Charnwood uses the latest

technology, including CNC controlled press brakes, robotic welders and laser profilers to ensure pinpoint accuracy and to provide the customer with a superior product. They have even installed their own vitreous enamelling plant. Vitreous enamel is the result of fusing powdered glass to a substrate and is durable, chemical resistant and flame retardant, as well as producing long-lasting colours, which allows Charnwood to manufacture stoves in a variety of shades to suit a kitchen's colour scheme.

So successful was this plant that it has become a business in its own right, enamelling goods like baths, non-Charnwood stoves and signage for companies and private customers.

A. J. Wells & Sons Ltd have also expanded into other areas of the stove-making industry, with Charnwood's sister company Anki Chimney Systems, which imports pumice chimneys made from Icelandic volcanic rock. These are ideal because they reduce heat loss, create better chimney drafts and there's less tar and soot build-up. They have also set up a fair-trade project called Bodj Products, which imports terracotta tiles and houseware goods from Cambodia, which is dedicated to developing Cambodia's local businesses.

Interesting fact: Charnwood's Cove 3 wood-burning stove has been included in Channel Four's *Grand Designs*.

Comitti of London

What they make:	clocks and barometers
Founder:	Onorato Comitti
Founded:	1850
Based:	London
Number of staff:	20

COMITTI OF London has been making clocks and barometers for over 150 years and base their designs on 350 years heritage of the craft in England. By adding a modern twist to traditional designs, they aim to provide quality-assured products that can compete in an ever-demanding marketplace – timeless products that compliment contemporary lifestyles.

The company was founded in 1850 by Onorato Comitti, a skilled Italian instrument-maker who came over to England in 1845 seeking to take advantage of the Industrial Revolution and the benefits it had on the economy. He established his workshops

in Clerkenwell, the centre of instrument making in London, and in a short time he was providing barometers and related instruments to discerning customers. In the late Victorian period the company expanded its product base into manufacturing clocks. Comitti of London remains a family-run company and is today run by the grandsons of George Barker, who married Louisa Comitti and became part of the business in the 1890s.

Comitti products reflect a unique heritage of making fine clocks and weather instruments in England. The industry was established in the 1650s, achieving a pre-eminence that remained unchallenged throughout the eighteenth and nineteenth centuries. In recent years Comitti have focused on making products that reflect the genius of eminent English clock-makers such as John Harrison, who created the world's first marine chronometer, which made it possible for seafarers to calculate their longitude position by observing the stars. Comitti's version of his 'Grasshopper' clock is modelled on the original that can be viewed today in the Royal Observatory in Greenwich, London.

Comitti employ an array of highly skilled craftsmen. Cabinet-makers create clock and barometer cases that feature solid woods, fine veneers and inlays. Each piece is hand rubbed and finished by polishers to enhance its natural beauty. Dial-makers hand assemble and paint the clock faces, skilled movement-makers

and instrument assemblers complete the final assembly and inspection. As well as all these, the skills of metal casters, glaziers, glassblowers and hand-makers are also required to create these beautiful and functional products. The company encourages customers to come and view their workshop, named The Clockworks, so they can see how they combine old craft skills with modern design. It is important to Comitti that their customers feel they are not just purchasing a clock or a barometer, but a real investment that will retain its intrinsic value throughout the years. To this end, some of the Comitti pieces are limited editions.

Whilst committed to retaining their roots, Comitti also understand the importance of remaining competitive by using modern innovation. Over the years they have made improvements to the clock mechanisms in the products they offer, including an automatic night silencer (a feature that silences the clock's chimes during the night hours) and precision quartz movements that are accurate to within a minute each year. The company has also developed temperature compensated aneroid barometer movements, which make it possible to provide local weather forecasts that are more accurate than national weather reports.

Interesting fact: The importance of clock-making and its vital contribution to society is summed up nicely by John Rushkin, the Victorian philosopher, who said, 'The clock is not merely the means of keeping the hours, but of synchronising the actions of men... the clock, not the steam engine, is the key machine of the industrial age.'

Conway Stewart

What they make: fountain pens
Founders: Frank Jarvis and Thomas Garner
Founded: 1905
Based: London
Number of staff: 15

CONWAY STEWART are purveyors of the finest fountain pens available. These handcrafted, elegant and beautiful yet functional fountain pens are a British classic. Conway Stewart pens have been used during historic moments, with Winston Churchill himself

using one during the war. To commemorate this, a range of pens named in his honour are often presented to foreign dignitaries on behalf of British politicians and royalty.

In 1905, Frank Jarvis and Thomas Garner created Conway Stewart Limited in Pasternoster Row, next to St Paul's Cathedral. The name probably derives from a famous vaudeville act of the day 'Conway and Stewart', a comedy duo that supposedly appeared at Collins Music Hall in Islington.

Conway Stewart has been upgraded many times to meet demands for its products, with its most significant move being in 1923 to 78/82 Shoe Lane in London, where the Conway Stewart factory and offices took up six floors and employed over 500 members of staff.

Conway Stewart pens have played an important role in both of the world wars. During World War One, they were invaluable to soldiers who wrote home to their loved ones and in World War Two, the Conway Stewart factory was converted into a munitions factory – it survived the Blitz, despite most of the buildings in the surrounding area being destroyed. During the war years, Conway Stewart continued to make a limited range of pens and their rationing of materials continued until the late 1940s when the company resumed its full manufacturing potential.

The company has produced some iconic pens, including the 'Dinkie' (the smallest practical fountain pen in the world). The business has also produced pens that celebrate anniversaries of the company, including the 1955 Conway Stewart No. 22 'Floral' for its Golden Jubilee, and the Conway Stewart 100, re-introduced for its centenary. Even today, the pens produced in the 1950s are eagerly snapped up by collectors who sometimes pay over a hundred times the original value of the pen.

The advent of cheap biros, ballpoint pens and mass production meant that in 1975 the company ceased production. This was not the end, however. The trademarks, designs and archives were kept intact and interest in their heritage continued. Like all great businesses, Conway Stewart adapted to the market and started to target collectors and lovers of fine pens, of the written word and those who appreciate timeless craftsmanship. Slowly but surely, the best pen-makers in Britain regained their mantle, and with some style.

In the 1990s the company released a range made from solid gold that now sell for upwards of £20,000. These wonderful pens also showcased great British craftsmen and women in various fields, including hand painting, enamelling and engraving. Today Conway Stewart has over 350 pens in seven different styles and over fifty colours; with prices ranging from £200 to £12,000, they are beautiful luxury gifts for retirement, birthdays, weddings and anniversaries, each one an individual masterpiece created with passion, knowledge and over one hundred years of experience.

Interesting fact: Tony Blair, George W. Bush, Bill Clinton, Her Majesty Queen Elizabeth II and The Duke of Edinburgh all own Conway Stewart pens.

Denby

What they make: pottery
Founder: William Bourne
Founded: 1809
Based: Denby, Derbyshire
Number of staff: 650

DERBYSHIRE HAS a long history of manufacturing pottery and the reason, predominantly, is the proximity of coal fields and clay deposits. In 1806, during the construction of a turnpike road from Alfreton to Derby, a seam of clay was uncovered in Denby.

The geology may dictate but visionaries are needed to capture the potential. One such was William Bourne. Summoned from a nearby pottery to examine the clay when it was discovered, William Bourne immediately grasped the individual and fine qualities of the Denby clay. He obtained a lease and Denby pottery was born. In 1809 William gave his son Joseph the task of running the pottery; he repaid his father's faith and started building an international reputation for quality bottles and jars to hold anything from ink, polish and medicines to preserves and ginger beer.

In the early days, from a single kiln, the focus was on craftsmanship and pride in the products, and Joseph's talent was quickly recognised. He was an ambitious businessman, but he was also an innovator and inventor of improved firing methods, kiln design and salt glaze techniques, and he set the tone for the next century of Denby.

Danesby Ware
ELECTRIC BLUE

**Joseph Bourne
& Son, Limited**
Denby Pottery, Nr. Derby

London Office & Showroom :
34, HOLBORN VIADUCT. E.C.1

Domestic cooking pots, bottles and jars were not the only output; Denby produced all manner of necessities. If it could be made out of clay then they would make it. In 1876, Alexander Graham Bell invented the telephone, and you may wonder what a pottery company could have to do with this; but Denby was foremost in the production of telegraph insulators.

The industrial revolution brought change. Glass became less expensive to produce and a more popular method of storage. Denby had to adapt, as all great businesses have to at some point in order to survive. Sadly many potteries in Derbyshire and neighbouring Nottinghamshire did not, and today very few still operate; but as cheaper, poorer quality products from overseas flood the British market, Denby stands firm. The company diversified by extending its kitchenware and developing the richly-coloured glazes which were to become its trademark. By the 1920s, Denby's pie dishes, jelly moulds, colanders and hot water bottles could be found in many homes along with vases and tobacco jars stamped 'Danesby Ware'.

Many of the companies in this book have had their histories altered by World War Two, and Denby is no different. Restrictions on coloured glaze stains and the demand for military teapots and bottles altered Denby's output. But after the war the company regained its stride and produced tableware and some of the most popular jugs, bowls, plates and cups available, many of which are collectors' items today.

The company prides itself on having 5,000 glazes, all harder than steel so that their tableware not only washes more easily but chips less readily. Each Denby piece passes through 25 pairs of hands during the production process before reaching yours, to ensure the best quality product makes it to your home.

Interesting fact: Salt glazing was a popular method of decorating stoneware in the early 1800s; common salt was thrown onto the kiln fires when the embers were at their hottest, and the salt vapour combined with the surface of the pot to produce a shiny brown surface coating.

Dri-Pak

What they make: traditional cleaning products
Founders: the Maxwell family
Founded: 1900
Based: Ilkeston, Derbyshire

DRI-PAK MAY not be the most glamorous British manufacturer, but they are single-handedly keeping alive a manufacturing process and creating a product that no other company on these shores makes – and one that deserves a successful comeback.

They are a family company which has been manufacturing traditional cleaning products since the early nineteenth century, the core products in their range including soda crystals, soap flakes, borax, bicarbonate of soda and white vinegar. In a world of hi-tech washing machines, branded washing powders and multi-million pound advertising campaigns selling consumers the smell of a Canadian wilderness or an alpine meadow, it is refreshing to see a British company making traditional products in a traditional manner without a vast cocktail of chemicals.

Dri-pak is now the only manufacturer of soap flakes and soda crystals in Great Britain. Before World War Two, soap flakes, a washboard and a mangle were the only way to do your washing. As the demand for biological washing powders took hold, however, the two big manufacturers Lever Brothers and ICI ceased production of their soap flakes and crystals and the entire market was left to Dri-pak. As the century rolled on and customer demand for well made, environmentally friendly cleaning products increased, more lines were added, strengthening the company and sowing the seeds for the success it is today.

The raw materials are sourced from the UK. Soda ash is extracted from limestone and primarily comes from the Peak District, a stone's throw from the factory. It is the growing concern for a more environmentally friendly way of life that is key to the future of this and many other British manufacturers. The popularity of TV shows such as *How Clean is your House?* is making consumers aware of the many chemicals in household cleaning products. Research has suggested chemical build-up (on work surfaces, for example, that come into contact with food) increases the allergies a child may suffer from and increases the possible onset of asthma, not to mention the damage to waterways when it is all flushed away. Toxic and caustic ingredients can cause irritation to the skin and eyes.

Soda crystals, borax, white vinegar, bicarbonate of soda and soap flakes are all biodegradable and cost effective – there's no cleaning or laundry task that can't be done by this range of products, and they can be safely combined (e.g. bicarbonate of soda and white vinegar mixed make scouring cream for cleaning tile grout). You can save money – and space in your cupboard. Dri-Pak offer downloadable information on how to get any cleaning job done with their products.

Traditional cleaning products are a real alternative to the commercial products of the superbrands that almost battled the

last remaining soap flake-maker into submission. They are safer, do not contain chlorine, phosphates, enzymes or bleach, are more cost effective and *really* won't cost you the earth.

Interesting fact: Soap flakes are still produced at Dri-Pak using the original flake-making machine which is now over 100 years old.

Ecos Organic Paint

What they make: organic, solvent-free paints
Founders: Ian West and John Ashworth
Founded: 1989
Based: Heysham, Lancashire

THE PAINTS which Ecos sell are currently the only range of paints in the world which do not contain *any* solvents or Volatile Organic Compounds (VOCs, which contribute to air pollution and global warming). This means that using them will reduce your carbon footprint not only because they are British-made, but because they do not release any greenhouse gases into the atmosphere. The use of paints worldwide emitted approximately 20–25 million tonnes of VOC into the atmosphere last year.

You may find, when painting or decorating, that you get a headache, your eyes sting, or you feel sick. This is due to the chemicals and solvents in the paint; all conventional gloss, matt and silk paints contain solvents, except Ecos Paints. Paints are a major contributor to indoor pollution – the air inside your house can be up to 70 times more polluted than that outside. The use of solvent-based paints is a major cause of Sick Building Syndrome, Danish Painter's Syndrome, asthma, allergies and chemical sensitivities.

As well as being free from solvents and VOCs, Ecos paints do not contain any white spirit, turpentine or formaldehyde. They are odour-free and contain no herbicides, pesticides, heavy metals or animal products – they are even entirely suitable for vegetarians and vegans (to paint their walls with – although

they're also non-toxic) and none are tested on animals. So you can use them in any place where you don't want unpleasant chemicals, like children's bedrooms or kitchens; and they're especially good if you have asthma or are allergic to some component of regular paint.

The paints were invented in 1989 by two scientists, one of whom suffered from ME (myalgic encephalomyelitis) and the other of whom had asthma. The range cost approximately one million pounds to develop, and after four years of weather-testing in both the UK and the USA, were put into commercial production in 1989. In addition to wall paints, Ecos make paints for wood (interior and exterior), varnishes and floor paints.

Ecos have also created other paints that are actively good for your health. Their anti-Electro Magnetic Radiation wall paint will shield your home from microwaves emitted from mobile phone masts and pylons, and they sell matt wall paint that will help insulate your walls and ceilings, again helping you to reduce your carbon footprint. But perhaps their most fascinating product is their 'Molecular Sieve' paint, which filters the air in your home and actually absorbs volatile toxic chemical pollutants. For instance, their anti-formaldehyde radiator paint absorbs much of the formaldehyde that most conventional radiators emit.

The molecular sieves look like clay or ceramic powder, and their molecules are tube-shaped, like macaroni; small molecules such as oxygen can pass in and out of the tube without difficulty, but larger molecules – such as those of VOCs – enter the tube but cannot leave, due to their size and molecular vibrations. Once absorbed, the trapped molecules are rendered harmless. It sounds like science fiction, but it really works.

Their prices compete well with ordinary paints, and you can even order online, get a free tester and often next day delivery. No wonder this small independent company has gathered a slew of accolades such as: *Which? Magazine* best environmentally friendly paint; Best Buy – Ethical Consumer; Daily Telegraph/Natwest Bank Clean technology Awards 1990; The Glaxo Welcome Responsible Business Award 1999; and the Millennium Marque 2000.

Interesting fact: Ecos paints are about 7,000 times purer than their closest competitor.

Mathmos

What they make: lava lamps and other light technologies
Founder: Edward Craven Walker
Founded: 1963
Based: Poole, Dorset and London
Number of staff: 15+

THE 1960S produced a cornucopia of style icons, at the pinnacle of which was the 'lava lamp'; a simple, hypnotic lamp that was as much part of the psychedelia of the decade as *Sgt Pepper's Lonely Hearts Club Band*, Ken Kesey and The Grateful Dead. For all its American symbolism, it was designed in Poole, Dorset where it is made to this day by British company, Mathmos.

The Astro Lamp, as it was known then, was conceived in the mind of Edward Craven-Walker, a former World War Two pilot,

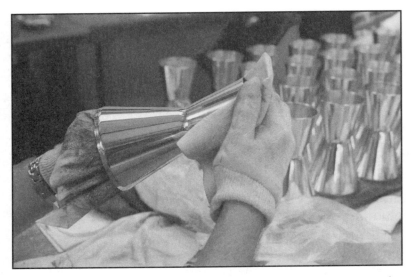

whilst he watched an egg timer in a pub in the New Forest. The device had a bubble that rose in water when the egg was boiled. The idea inspired Craven-Walker and he spent the next few years developing a formula for a lamp that harnessed the cooling and heating of wax in liquid.

On its release the lamp soon became fashionable, adorning film sets, bedsits and university halls the world over. As the 1970s gave way to the 1980s, however, the zeitgeist moved on and sales of the lamp collapsed. Edward Craven-Walker disappeared into obscurity and it was not until 1989 that Cressida Granger and David Mulley resurrected the design.

Cressida and David had been selling lamps and assorted vintage lighting with moderate success around the UK but it was Cressida who saw the potential of the 'lava lamp', and the two set about buying the rights from Craven-Walker. It took them five years to obtain 100 per cent of the company, which they renamed Mathmos in 1992, with Craven-Walker remaining a consultant until he passed away in 2000. It is well documented how fashion comes in cycles and it was the vision of a British company that seized the opportunity and turned it into a global success.

The next ten years were tremendous and saw Mathmos double in size every year. The fashion for all things retro and 1960s catapulted sales. In 1999 David left the company and Cressida took complete control. Although the lava lamp was the foundation on which the company was built, it is in no way the only product manufactured by Mathmos, indeed it is just the tip of the illuminated iceberg.

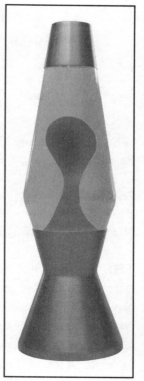

The company ethos turned to innovation and design. New light technologies such as the Airswitch™ (whereby the light is controlled by moving your hand in the air above the source) and Mathmos Mobiles™ have seen Mathmos move to the forefront of light invention, used and admired globally. Working alongside exciting designers such as Azumi and Ross Lovegrove means Mathmos can continue to build beautiful and engaging lights that, like the original Lava Lamp, will stand the test of time.

Mathmos has won two Queen's Awards for Export, with Cressida Granger reaching the final of the Veuve Cliquot businesswoman of the year. The future is bright.

Interesting fact: The name Mathmos comes from the film *Barberella* and refers to the bubbling force below the fictional city of Sogo.

Newey and Bloomer

What they make: Simplex kettles
Founders: Frederick Charles Moore Bloomer and
Herbert Richard Newey
Founded: 1850
Based: Birmingham, West Midlands
Number of staff: 25

THE MAKERS of Simplex kettles received an e-mail not long after Hurricane Katrina from a customer in New Orleans. The lady in question had put her kettle on to boil just before her whole street was destroyed by the hurricane. She forgot about her kettle, which was ruined by the time she came back to it. Newey & Bloomer understood it was the little day-to-day things that mattered most, and sent her a new one. So says the 'kettle queen' who has worked at Newey & Bloomer for over twelve years and receives hundreds of e-mails from customers all over the world with stories and even photos of their Simplex kettles. Some people have owned one for over thirty years, and send it back to the factory for a new handle or simply a polish.

Newey and Bloomer first designed and manufactured the Simplex copper kettle in 1903. The business was originally established in 1850 by Birmingham-born gentlemen Bloomer and Newey, who began by manufacturing an assortment of barbershop fittings, bar tops, bed warming pans and washing possors and used their copper expertise to manufacture this most necessary of kitchen appliances. The design and patent for the Simplex whistling kettle,

the Simplex energy saving model and the brand name Simplex came in 1935. Newey & Bloomer continued to manufacture the Simplex as five generations of the Bloomer family passed through the factory doors. In January 2005, Mark Bloomer, great-grandson of founder Frederick, sold the business to another family-run company, GB Metal Spinnings, but the company has continued to go from strength to strength, exporting across America especially. The Simplex Beehive from the 1950s was re-launched just six years ago and is proving a hit.

Simplex kettles are manufactured entirely by hand from solid copper (even chrome-plated versions start out as natural copper), which is malleable enough to be manipulated into almost any shape – hence the quite unmistakable look of a Simplex kettle. Copper is also a superb conductor of heat, which makes Simplex kettles the perfect vessels for saving energy: the range of kettles with a coil on the bottom actually retain their heat so effectively that water is boiled up to 25 per cent faster than their flat bottomed counterparts. Just think of the difference if every time a kettle was boiled, a quarter of the energy could be saved.

Every kettle is tested up to 20 times to ensure quality and consistency. The Simplex kettle is an iconic design and is flying the flag for manufacturing in the Midlands. The kettles promoted so many years ago for their energy-saving qualities ('Energy is Expensive – Save It') are proving just as popular in today's environmentally-conscious world.

Interesting fact: Simplex kettles have appeared in many Hollywood films, including *Psycho*, *The Colour of Money*, *Steel Magnolias* and *Meet the Parents*.

Roberts Radio

What they make: radios
Founders: Harry Roberts and Leslie Bidmead
Founded: 1932
Based: Mexborough, Yorkshire
Number of staff: 30

BRITAIN PRODUCED many wireless transmitters in the early days of radio, and while today so many radios are produced in the Far East, Roberts Radio is still manufacturing their famous radios on British soil.

Harry Roberts was born on 20 May 1910 in Mile End, London, the youngest of six children. When he left school, Harry would have liked to follow his older brother Charles into the transport industry, but couldn't afford the £40 needed to buy a second-hand lorry and so opted to go and work for the Rees Mace Manufacturing Company instead – one of the many small manufacturers catering for the thriving market in wireless sets since broadcasting had begun in the early twentieth century. Rees Mace specialised in 'portables', although they were still far too bulky to move around much; other types of receiver always had to be connected to an outdoor or 'frame' aerial. It was here that Harry first became interested in portable radios, which were becoming popular among those who could afford them.

Shortly after, Harry left Rees Mace and joined Pell, Cahill & Company where he was responsible for adjusting wireless radios and correcting faults. With a good reference he left in 1927 as

the company went into liquidation and joined up with freelance salesman Richard R. Bennett, who had been Cahill's service manager; Bennett contacted prospective customers, and Harry's role was collecting receivers from suppliers and demonstrating them to potential customers. Harry was soon to meet the man with whom he would found Roberts Radio.

Leslie Bidmead, five years older than Harry, had been a radio enthusiast since his schooldays. In 1923, using a home-made two-valve receiver, he picked up an American station called WGY, with reception loud enough to be audible 40 metres from the loudspeaker, and clear enough for him to have his feat confirmed. Bidmead had established a receiver manufacturing company, but through a combination of illicit sidelines by his partner and withheld payments by a major customer, it had to close. It was the company's landlord who suggested that in order to pay off arrears in rent, Bidmead join forces with Harry Roberts. In November 1932, the company became the 'Roberts Radio Company', and soon after the two business partners married two sisters, Leslie and Elsie.

By 1936, Roberts were marketing their 'Midget Portable', which at under one foot square was able to receive all the principal European stations, was ideal for the home, the car, picnics and holidays, and came with a six-month guarantee. Early receivers were in suitcase format, with loudspeaker and aerial in the lid. In 1946, the Roberts P4D, priced 14 guineas plus tax, was displayed at the 'Britain Can Make It' exhibition in London, still the least well-known of the brands displayed. The company's growth has been steady rather than spectacular, but over the next 75 years Roberts radios became icons of our times and the benchmark by which all portable radios are measured. Receiving royal warrants to the Prince of Wales and the Queen, their pedigree is unmatched, as is their British style.

They have embraced the future of broadcasting, building the first portable DAB digital radio in 1999 and strengthening their digital output. When the analogue receivers are finally turned off, Roberts Radio will have progressed with the times and Harry Roberts will be able to rest soundly, with more radio stations to choose from than he could have ever possibly imagined.

Interesting fact: In 1959, at two weeks' notice, Roberts provided a compact, battery-powered, short-wave set for the Cambridge Colombian Expedition, to be carried about on a pack-mule and exposed to extremes of altitude, temperature and humidity.

Relyon Ltd

What they make:	beds and mattresses
Founders:	the Price family
Founded:	1858
Based:	Wellington, Somerset
Number of staff:	517

PRICE BROTHERS began its life as a wool merchant back in 1858, founded by the Price family. However, the family soon saw a more appealing opportunity – the very comfortable world of beds. In 1935, they changed their name to Relyon, and they're certainly making a comfortable profit nowadays – as the market

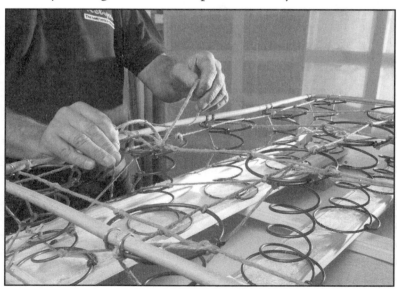

leader for high quality mattresses, divan sets, storabeds and bedframes, with prestigious awards from organisations such as the Worshipful Company of Furniture Makers in the City of London.

In 1966, Relyon became a public company, and in 2001 was acquired by Steinhoff International Holdings Ltd, a South African group. The backing of this multifaceted organisation has allowed Relyon to prosper further,

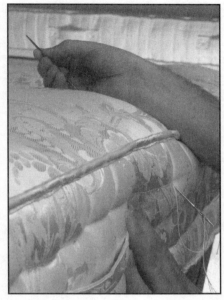

associating with other UK companies such as Pritex, a foam and fibre products business and Steinhoff UK furniture. The group owns factories around the world, and not all of Relyon's large and extensive product list is made in Britain – but all their mattress and divan ranges are made at their Wellington and Okehampton sites, and their handmade brass bedsteads and headboards, and occasional furniture is made at their Bridport site.

Their mattresses contain the most sumptuous of fillings for ultimate night-time relaxation, with specially designed versions to suit those customers who need an anti-allergenic variety. Craftsmanship details include pocketed springs – with linen cord threaded through to tie them together, leaving each spring free to respond to the contours of the body. Quality fibres allow the mattress to breathe. A feature of many Relyon mattresses is the stitched sides that extend the sleeping area to the very edge of the mattress by supporting the mattress walls. This also ensures the necessary rigidity and strength of the mattress for many years.

The Relyon brand can be found in all leading furniture stores in the UK, firmly established as by far the most significant supplier to the top half of the UK market, as well as supplying to overseas customers.

Interesting fact: Relyon started out as a wool merchant in Wellington, Somerset.

The Hill Brush Company Ltd

What they make: brooms, hygiene brushes and
equestrian brushes
Founders: Fred and Bill Coward
Founded: 1922
Based: Mere, Wiltshire
Number of staff: 115

THE HILL Brush Company Ltd is a family-owned business
started in 1922 by Fred and Bill Coward. Born in 1897 and 1899,
they both falsified their ages in order to join the services in World
War One, but then returned to Mere and started making brushes

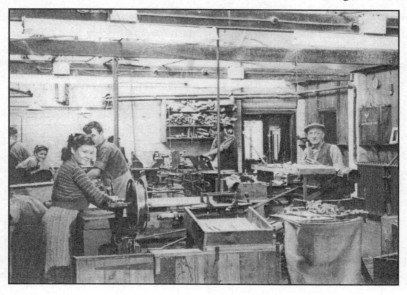

in a small workshop on the premises of their father's wood turnery business, borrowing money from family to set up. They were subsequently joined by their respective sons David and Richard, and today David's sons Philip and Martin run the company whilst Richard's son Peter runs their subsidiary company in the USA (Baltimore).

Philip's daughter Clare has worked for the company, and his son Charles has joined the company in the sales and marketing department.

The Company originally specialised in dairy and agricultural brushes, and within a few years many of the streets from Hampshire to Cornwall were being swept with brushes that had been made by Hill Brush. They also produced brushes for milk bottles and were one of only two manufacturers of this type of brush outside the United States, exporting them to many parts of the world. At this time all the brushes were made by hand. The business grew, and in 1927 moved to Lordsmead Mill, a disused silk mill, where the waterwheel provided power for the drills that bored holes in the brush stocks.

Automatic brush-making machines were introduced in the 1930s and now the company uses some of the most advanced brush-making machinery available. Their latest computer controlled production machine will fill 1,000 tufts per minute into the brushes. They manufacture over three million brushes per annum and sell to over 1,000 customers in over forty countries worldwide. The company has been a royal warrant holder since 1981. Throughout its lifetime, the main objective of the Hill Brush Company Ltd has been to provide its customers with very high quality brushes at reasonable prices. Some of the workforce are the third generation of their families to be employed by the company.

Like so many British manufacturers, Hill Brush are masters of innovation. Have you ever struggled to open an oyster? Hill Brush was approached by a company who had an idea of how to overcome this rather unusual predicament. They developed the idea and now manufacture a wooden oyster clamp that fits on the edge of your dining table and allows you to open your oyster with the minimum of effort – which is now sold to restaurants and hotels across the UK.

The company is committed to a policy which is sympathetic to environmental issues, and strives to minimise the environmental impact at all stages of production and where possible uses environmentally harmonious components. For instance, all of the natural vegetable fibres used by the company are harvested, and the gathering and processing of these fibres helps to support many local communities in developing countries. The company is unique in having its own brush fibre-dressing department which was started in 1926, and now processes all types of natural fibres from many parts of the world including Sierra Leone, India, Sri Lanka, Indonesia, Mexico, China, Lesotho and Brazil. The fibre-dressing department enables the company to offer special mixtures at short notice.

Interesting fact: One of the first members of staff employed in 1927 at the age of 14 became chief foreman and served the company until his retirement in 1978.

Wesley-Barrell

What they make: upholstery furniture
Founder: Anthony Ernest Barrell
Founded: 1895
Based: Witney, Oxfordshire
Number of staff: 120

ANTHONY ERNEST Barrell, a farmer's son, was branch manager of Walter J. Valentine, a business in Potton, Befordshire. He later purchased the business of Augustus G. Harris in Witney and it was renamed Valentine and Barrell. It sold furniture, glass, household equipment and footwear, as well as offering an undertaker's and funeral carriage service, and furniture-making, carpentry and upholstery departments.

Anthony had five children, and in order to try and provide for their future, he broke with the Valentine family and started a business of his own, specialising in beds, quilts and mattresses. Anthony's oldest son died of wounds sustained in World War One, but his younger son, Wesley, survived serious injuries, and with his wife he established his own firm, Wesley-Barrell Mail Order Bed and Bedding Makers, which became Wesley-Barrell (Witney) Ltd in 1934. Anthony's company was sold in 1933 when he retired, and the present company has developed from Wesley's mail order business, initially under the management of his son Peter, who joined the firm in 1954 as a young man in the workshops.

Now, of the six current directors, three are Peter's daughters, and great-granddaughters of Anthony. None of them originally set out to join the firm, but were invited to do so by their father, who tried to find places within the company that would utilise his daughters' talents to the fullest degree. He also opened the first Wesley-Barrell showroom in 1960, realising that people liked to see the products for themselves before buying, and also seeking to be able to deal more directly with the public. The first showroom was opened in Bridge Street, Witney – adjacent to the company's workshops.

Wesley-Barrell has had to work hard to throw off its more traditional image; it is not widely known that it has been using natural materials – cotton, wool felt, or even real hair – rather than exclusively using foam in its sofa padding for 25 years, anticipating the current trend for environmentally friendly goods. Wesley-Barrell's sofas may be based on classic English styles, but every piece is bespoke, so they can tailor a sofa for your living room to suit your needs exactly.

All sofas are constructed by hand, and no two are the same. Sofa frames are completely handmade from carefully seasoned woods, and have a ten-year guarantee. The springs are sewn into the sofa by hand, and the company offers literally thousands of fabrics to make the sofa covering. Many traditional furniture-making skills of a century ago are still employed in the construction of Wesley-Barrell products, while other necessary techniques have been refined and improved in the last 30 years, incorporating modern developments such as the computer aided fabric cutting system.

The company is very keen to encourage and help preserve traditional crafts, and to that end it has recently set up the Wesley-Barrell Craft Awards in association with the Crafts Council to recognise home-grown talent. These have two categories, one for furniture and one for vessels; the prize on offer is £3,000 and a place on a business mentoring scheme.

Wesley-Barrell have 16 showrooms nationwide. They are one of the few companies that offer a renovation service on their own products, encouraging longevity and a sofa that will last a lifetime. They are also expanding into interior design advice, home accessories and dining room furniture.

Interesting fact: Anthony Barrell started out as a coffin-maker.

Getting Around

A Third Foot

What they make: skateboards
Founders: Ken and Joel
Founded: 1997
Based: Birmingham, West Midlands
Number of staff: 4 (plus riders)

FOR THOSE that skate, it is a passion – a part of your life, culture and identity to be celebrated. In the architecture within which they live, skaters see infinite possibility and British skateboard manufacturer A Third Foot makes it possible with their handcrafted British decks.

In early 1997, Ken and Joel went to The Prince's Trust with a business plan and were awarded funding. The market was dominated by US made decks, and it was widely believed and often suggested (by US companies) that only US made decks were any good. Ken and Joel believed otherwise and proceeded to prove it. Now, US manufacturing dominance has been replaced by that of China, due to its cheap labour, but A Third Foot is still highly regarded and seen as a benchmark by which European decks are judged.

The manufacturing technique that has been mastered, improved on and perfected is a fine process done mostly by hand that ensures every skateboard leaves the workshop with perfect pop and sound structural integrity. The best wood produces a consistent, more springy pop. Canadian hard maple is cut into seven rectangular sheets which are sanded and dyed. The seven plies are stuck together using glue and a special catalyst which binds the wood, and are then pressed – pressure and temperature are monitored to retain consistency. The boards are left to cure for three weeks, so that they fuse together giving durability and strength.

A THIRD FOOT

Finally, the skateboard is shaped, drilled and bandsawn using a shape template. It is sanded and given a final cure before being sprayed with lacquer. Graphics are then developed by the art team and screen-printed on. The boards are then shrink-wrapped and shipped to suppliers. Then the streets ring out to the unmistakable sound of maple on concrete from British-made skateboards.

A Third Foot also produces a range of screen-printed T-shirts and stickers, also made on-site. Over thirty skateboard suppliers stock their products, but they are keen to champion Skater Owned Shops, or SOS – they plan to develop a good-quality SOS board at a competitive price which they will offer to all such shops, hoping it will bridge the gap between cheap imported boards and more expensive British-made products. A Third Foot are helping to keep the skating subculture alive in Britain; hopefully, British skaters will be using their boards for a long time to come.

Interesting fact: 21 June is national skateboarding day

Alex Moulton Bicycles

What they make:	bicycles
Founder:	Dr Alex Moulton
Founded:	1958
Based:	Bradford on Avon, Wiltshire

DR ALEX Moulton first became interested in cycling efficiency during the Suez Crisis in 1956; petrol rationing meant that low-energy forms of transport were more necessary than ever before. He dreamed of creating a bicycle that any adult could ride which was also 'more pleasurable to have and more effective to use' than any other. It should allow a normal riding position, be

lightweight and open for ease of access, and have luggage-carrying facilities. Meeting all these requirements was quite difficult, but after intensive research, it was concluded that such a bicycle could be made if it had small wheels with high pressure tyres, full suspension, and a frame that was as stiff as possible. The unique design of the Moulton bicycle was born.

Smaller wheels provide a number of advantages; they allow faster acceleration because they are lighter, the shorter spokes mean that they are stronger, the drag on the bike is reduced because of the smaller area of the wheels, there is greater stability due to a lowered centre of gravity, and more luggage can be carried further down. The gears on an Alex Moulton bicycle are chosen to match the size of the wheels, meaning that riding is no more difficult than on a conventional bicycle. Full suspension means that the bicycle is more comfortable to ride and there is less strain on the wheels.

The frame on an Alex Moulton bicycle is much stronger than a regular frame and, because the crossbar is much lower, it can be ridden by cyclists of any height or gender, or even by elderly or disabled riders. The stiffness of the frame means that none of the rider's energy is wasted in flexing the frame.

Because Moulton bicycles are unique, all their parts and fixtures must be produced in-house, including the rubber suspension and moulds for Moulton tyres. The forks and the frames are hand-brazed by company craftsmen. The focus is very much on quality and function – some Alex Moulton bicycles have been ridden for over 50,000 miles.

Moulton bicycles are generally more compact

than the average bicycle, and on many of them, the frame can be separated for greater portability. The New Series Moulton splits into five pieces. Moulton handlebars are adjustable, meaning that the bicycle can be used for racing, touring, or just having fun.

Dr Moulton's bicycles quickly became a success in the athletic world; their superior handling and acceleration meant that they were especially successful on the track in pursuit events. Today, racing cyclists must all compete on similar vehicles, so Dr Moulton has focused on supplying vehicles for record-breaking and distance attempts. For instance, in 1970–1, Colin Martin rode an F-frame Moulton from England to Australia, and in 1997 Ben Steele, Oliver Mathew and Baz Bix used Moulton APBs to ride across the Gobi Desert. Now that low-energy forms of transport are more vital than ever, Dr Moulton's contributions to the world of cycling can only be a good thing.

Interesting fact: David Bogdan completed the Race Across America – the longest annual endurance cycle event in the world – in 1987 and 1988, riding an Alex Moulton Jubilee bike. In 1988 he finished eighth out of 35, covering over 3,000 miles in ten days, 15 hours and one minute.

Bennington Carriages

What they make: carriages
Founder: Michael Mart
Founded: 1967
Based: Newark, Nottinghamshire
Number of staff: 15

BENNINGTON CARRIAGES, although only 40 years old, is part of the long-running British tradition of horse-drawn carriages and what began as a project to provide exercise for a pet pony has led to four decades of quality manufacturing.

Michael Mart, the founder of Bennington Carriages, started out as an engineering apprentice in Nottingham, but when he finished

his apprenticeship, he and his wife Margaret decided to move to the country. In 1964, they set up home in the village of Long Bennington, Lincolnshire and from there Michael founded Artistic Iron Products Ltd, a company that specialised in making wrought-iron gates, horseboxes, trailers and carrying out agricultural repairs. Artistic Iron Products Ltd was later to become the parent company for Bennington Carriages.

When his two daughters, Sue and Wendy, were children, the family owned a Shetland pony that was reluctant to let anyone ride it, and with a view to providing the pony with some exercise, Michael designed his first carriage. Seeing how well this carriage worked, it was not long before Michael decided to expand his business into designing professional horse-driving carriages, often competing in horse-driving trials in his own revolutionary designs.

Horse-driving trials or combined driving is an equestrian sport using carriages and has three stages; presentation, dressage and marathon, which are designed to test all aspects of the horses and carriage. Whereas other competitors were racing in carriages designed for leisure riding, with high backs that were vulnerable to tipping over, Michael, with his engineering background, made carriages that were designed for speed and off-road durability, required for the last stage of the competition. He was the first carriage-maker to introduce the back step to his carriages that allowed the groom to stand, helping to provide balance, and also the first to pioneer aluminium wheels, which were lighter and stronger than the traditionally used wooden wheels.

It wasn't long before Michael's carriages got him noticed by other competitors, including the Duke of Edinburgh, who at the time was drawing up the rules for horse-driving trials. So impressed was Prince Phillip by Michael's carriages that in 1979 he issued Bennington Carriages with a royal warrant to become his official carriage-maker, which the company still holds to this day.

Producing up to 150 carriages a year from their original factory in Lincolnshire, Bennington has become renowned for its quality, attention to detail and customer service and has a varied client base, from Disney World, Florida to the Sultan of Brunei. They remain the forerunner of innovative carriage design and

are constantly maintaining the delicate balance between modernising and retaining the traditional methods of carriage building. By doing this, they have developed a range of 30 carriages that include both professional racing carriages and amateur carriages, with the Marts keen to remember where the business stemmed from.

Carriages are mainly owned by enthusiasts who pursue the sport either professionally or for pleasure. One of the Bennington carriages, the Fun Bug, was controversial when it was first launched, as it was made specifically for newcomers and those who just want to enjoy carriage driving. Since then it has become one of their most successful carriages, with orders even being placed for it in the USA. The Mart family, as expert drivers, are always ready to test-drive their own products. While Michael still continues to enhance and improve the carriages, his daughter Sue, now the managing director of the company, uses them to compete on a national level, helping to further promote the Bennington name with her many successes. With this, the owners of Bennington Carriages are able to better understand what a carriage needs in order to be first class.

Interesting fact: The Cinderella wedding carriage used at Disney World, Florida was designed and manufactured by Bennington Carriages.

Caterham Cars

What they make:	cars
Founder:	Colin Chapman
Founded:	1957
Based:	Caterham, Surrey
Number of staff:	70

ORIGINALLY CREATED by Colin Chapman and launched as the Lotus 7 back in 1957, the Caterham has since gone on to become the benchmark against which all kit cars are measured. Across much of Britain, and increasingly, France, Germany, Japan and Sweden, the deep, penetrating growl of the 1,999 cc, four cylinder, 210 b.h.p. engine can be heard tearing up race tracks, setting track records and scaring the life out of first-time drivers.

Caterham had been involved in development and sales of the Lotus 7 since 1959. When, in the summer of 1973, the Lotus

company planned to end production of the Lotus 7, Caterham took on manufacturing rights to it – a decision which would prove momentous. Three decades later, they have generated nearly 50 different interpretations of the Lotus 7 and made over 11,000 sales. Perhaps one of their most popular moves, in 2001, was to provide an extra few inches in the leg and side to give the modern driver a more comfortable ride – definitely a good idea, considering the original Lotus 7 was built around Chapman's 5'6" physique. Then, in 2004, Caterham produced what could be the biggest overhaul of the Lotus 7 yet – the Cosworth-powered CSR model, which accelerated from 0 to 60 mph in just 3.1 seconds.

Colin Chapman had always believed that engineering out unnecessary weight was vital to successful car design. Caterham have stuck by this belief and it is the lightweight body of their cars, combined with a highly tuned engine, that gives almost super-car performance to a vehicle that you can build in your garage for well under £20,000. All design, manufacturing and parts are sourced from the British Isles, making Caterham one of the last remaining true beacons of the British car industry. There are eight official designs in the current Lotus 7 family, but no two Caterham cars are exactly the same – and with every customer being different, why should they be? One of the most talked about models has been the Superlight R500, first seen in 1999. It was the fastest production car built for many years, going from 0 to 60 mph in 3.4 seconds and able to go from 0 to 100 to 0 mph in less than 10 seconds.

The history of Caterham is steeped in motor sport accolades; so much so that in the 1970s it was actually banned from racing due to its vast superiority over rivals. This was a blessing in disguise for Caterham as it inspired them to set up single-make races, which incorporated strict regulations to minimise cost and produce close, exciting races.

Caterham also reinvented motor sport for the novice with the groundbreaking Caterham Academy, which enters its twelfth

year in 2007. Quite simply, a novice with no race experience can buy a road-legal Caterham, receive race tuition and compete in a special beginner's championship over the course of the year. The Academy concept has created over 600 new racing drivers and demand continues to outstrip supply year after year. Caterham's 1973 decision hasn't just been good for them, but for motor sports as a whole.

Interesting fact: Their R400 model, the latest in a long line of pure racing-bred British sportscars with a top speed of 140 mph, does 0–60 in 3.8 seconds, well into supercar performance territory.

Clews Competition Machines (CCM)

What they make: motorbikes
Founder: Alan Clews
Founded: 1971
Based: Bolton, Lancashire
Number of staff: 12

THINK MOTORBIKES, and you might think of Honda, Yamaha or Suzuki. But if you thought you couldn't buy British when it came to motorbikes, think again – or just think of CCM. Founded by Alan Clews in 1971, this company still manufactures its products in Britain, putting together a range of bikes to incredibly exacting standards.

Alan Clews initially trained as a weighing machine mechanic, but after stealing a ride on a colleague's bike, he became hooked on motorcycle trial riding. By the early 1960s he was attempting to put together a bike on his own, focusing on keeping the centre of gravity low and making sure the handling was good. His weighing machine training came in very handy here – after all, it's all about balance when you're on a motorbike. He began to compete in trials using bikes that he'd tuned and set up himself, and soon other riders started to ask him to build or modify their machines as well.

He was looking to widen his field of work, and so when the company BSA was selling off a chunk of its stock he took the opportunity to buy a truckload of competition parts cheap. The first Clews bike had a production run of seven, but demand quickly surpassed this. Within a few months, Clews had set up a formal company structure and was producing bikes made from his own frames, with other parts contracted from outside suppliers.

Clews wished to be able to tailor each machine to fit its rider's need. By the end of 1972, he had sold 42 machines, all built by him, and the company was gathering momentum; with their machines, Jack Mathews came first in the British side-car trials championship in 1973, and the champion CCM rider Vic Allan reached the top three in both the Swiss and Luxembourg 500cc Grands Prix. By 1976, over sixty people were employed at the workshop to meet demand, and in one year the company delivered more than 2,000 bikes. They had a wide range of customers, including the Bombardier Corporation of Canada (who required 4,000 bikes) and even the Sultan of Oman (who requested 54 for his display team). CCM's MT 500 model was supplied to the British, Canadian and Jordan armies, solely by CCM, and over 3,000 were sold before

Harley Davidson bought the rights to the design and took it to the US.

In 1998, Alan Clews and his son Austin sold their majority share in the company to Peter Swift and Co. It seemed that the company was going from strength to strength: in 2002, CCM R30 models were used to do wheelies down The Mall during the Queen's Jubilee Parade, and in 2003, CCM made it to the big screen when the film *Lara Croft: Tomb Raider* was released, its eponymous heroine riding a CCM 644. However, behind the scenes things were not looking so positive, and in July 2004, CCM was forced to close its doors due to mounting debts. For a while, all seemed lost, but then, miraculously, Alan Clews, his son Austin and his son-in-law Gary Harthern managed to buy back the company and all its assets.

CCM claim they can supply their customers with the highest quality bikes available, and with their experience, they certainly understand the needs of the British biker. After their miraculous rise, fall and rise again, let's hope this most British of companies stays on the road, riding on into a glorious future.

Interesting fact: In 1976, Eddie Kidd made his first ever televised motorcycle jump over 13 double-decker buses riding a CCM bike.

Coachman Caravan Company

What they make: caravans
Founded: 1986
Based: Hull, Yorkshire
Number of staff: 135

MOST OF us have been on a caravan holiday at some point. It attracts people from all walks of life, from young families on their first holiday to retired couples who wish to spend their twilight years in comfort. After all, caravanning is one of the most economic alternatives for those people who cannot afford to go abroad each year. The caravans designed by Coachman Caravan Company cater to people of all ages, lifestyles and budgets. Since 2004, the company has won 11 first place awards for quality and design. So, as their advertising says, 'In a Coachman caravan you can relax and

enjoy life, because relaxing is something we, at Coachman, never do.'

Formed in 1986, with their first line of VIP caravans on the market in 1987, Coachman was recognised early on for its excellence with its VIP 500/4 winning the Tourer of the Year Award in 1988. Since then Coachman has consistently won awards and

acclaim from respectable names in the caravanning community, including *Caravan Magazine* and The Caravan Club.

Since it was established, Coachman has weathered many ups and downs in the market, including an acquisition that incorporated Coachman into a wider group, before a manager buyout reinstated the company to its independent status. They have also successfully overcome hostile exchange rates to become part of the export market. All this has not affected staff loyalty, and Coachman enjoys a low staff turnover, with many employees coming from the same family groups. To improve training and skills within the company, Coachman offers its staff in-house training programmes that are endorsed by the GMB Union (the National General Trade Union). As well as this, Coachman are organising their first formal apprenticeship programme, which will allow the company to pass on its skills to the next generation.

Coachman uses computer manufacturing systems, amongst the most advanced on the market, to build the best quality caravans possible. With this efficient system in place, Coachman predicts that by 2010 they will have increased their production from 1,700 units per annum to 2,500, securing 10 per cent of the new tourer caravan market.

Coachman offers four ranges of caravan: Amara, Pastiche, VIP and Laser with 20 models available within these ranges to choose from. Each of these models is designed to provide comfort at affordable prices.

Quality and reliability are paramount; the manufacturing stage of each caravan is carefully monitored by four inspectors, and comprehensive pre-shipping tests are carried out before the caravans hit the market. With water ingress and de-lamination guarantees for up to six years, and a manufacturer's warranty for three years as standard, Coachman provides great after-purchase service too.

Interesting fact: They have their own Coachman Owners Club, founded in 1993, which allows the purchasers of their caravans to meet up for socials and rallies, creating a sense of community amongst their customers.

Cosworth

What they make:	performance engines and performance engine components
Founders:	Mike Costin and Keith Duckworth
Founded:	1958
Based:	Northampton, Northamptonshire
Number of staff:	150+

IF YOU build motor car engines and put them in cars whose sole *raison d'être* is to go faster for longer than other cars in the race, then how successful you are can be judged by the races you win. A book could be filled with races that Cosworth engines have won. They are top of the field and they are made in Britain by British engineers.

When the Formula One cars lined up on the grid at any race in the 2006 season, it was widely acknowledge that the best engine was the Cosworth, which could rev up to a unrivalled 20,000 rpm. That year, Williams were using a Cosworth V8 engine and Scuderia Toro Rosso were using a Cosworth rev-limited V10. Back in 1978, 15 teams used Cosworth engines and in 1969 Cosworth-powered cars won every Grand Prix, a feat that was repeated in 1973. During the 1970s Jackie Stewart, Emerson Fittipaldi and James Hunt all won Formula One championships and Nelson Piquet won three times in the 1980s using Cosworth engines. Only Ferrari have won more races and no one has supplied more teams. Quite a record from a company that only started in 1958 and then only from a small London workshop.

Mike Costin and Keith Duckworth had a dream: their passion was engines and they wanted to create the best in the world. Their skill was such that their London workshop soon became too small and they relocated to north London where they began work on the Ford 105E engine. In 1960 they tasted their first success when Jim Clarke took a win in the Formula junior category.

By the mid 1960s the company had moved to Northampton where the foundations would be laid for F1 and motor sport domination with the creation of the legendary DFV engine. Mike and Keith produced an engine which in its pure and subsequent guises clinched 155 races and dominated the sport for 15 years.

The company has been through numerous owners, and in 1998 it was split into two companies: Cosworth Technology – sold to the Mahle Group in 2004 – and Cosworth Racing, owned by Ford for several years and recently sold to Champ Car World Series owners Gerald Forsythe and Kevin Kalkhoven.

Cosworth leverages its successful motor sport pedigree, performance technology expertise and globally recognised brand to provide high quality engineered solutions for a growing customer base. The company's head office in Northampton is home to leading

edge engineering, world class manufacturing and comprehensive test facilities. In addition to the traditional markets, Cosworth is engaged in designing and developing engines and components for marine, locomotive and aerospace applications. With a strong portfolio of engineering contracts in place, Cosworth's rich and varied history is set to continue as the company approaches its fiftieth anniversary.

Interesting fact: Seven times world champion Michael Schumacher won his first Grand Prix in a Cosworth Powered Benetton.

Griffon Hovercraft Ltd (GHL)

What they make: hovercraft
Founder: Dr Edwin Gifford
Founded: 1976
Based: Southampton, Hampshire
Number of staff: 45

WHEN YOU think of a hovercraft, what springs to mind? Perhaps you might have nostalgic memories of bobbing across the Solent in one as a child on holiday, or find them fun because of their huge inflated cushions. Yet, there is so much more to the humble hovercraft than meets the eye.

Back in 1959, British engineer Christopher Cockerell (later Sir Christopher) invented the hovercraft – a combination of aircraft

and marine technology. It was
a breakthrough in engineering.
For the first time we had a mode
of transport that could conquer
land or water with equal ease.

In 1964, test pilot Don
Robertson and structural engineer Dr Edwin Gifford were asked
by Cockerell to set up the world's first commercial hovercraft
company, Hovertravel Ltd. Since then the company's hovercraft
have carried some 25 million passengers. Still involved with
Hovertravel Ltd, but wanting to create smaller, inexpensive and
more simply produced hovercraft, Dr Gifford founded Griffon
Hovercraft Ltd (GHL) in 1976.

As opposed to Hovertravel Ltd's gas turbine engines, GHL
developed hovercraft with petrol and then diesel-powered engines
– a world first for small to medium-sized hovercraft. In the 1980s,
they drove technology forward with innovations such as ducted
propellers, skirt shift systems and low noise propellers. With the
craft no longer needing to be flown and maintained by aircraft
pilots and engineers, Gifford managed to lower the costs and open
up a whole new market.

In 1984, the first diesel-engine Griffon was named the
Griffon 1000TD (1,000 kgs payload). This ten-seat model is
still produced and used today, though numerous other models
have now been developed – all the way up to the top of the
range, the Griffon 8100TD, with a 12 tonne payload that
carries 98 passengers.

Griffon Hovercraft Ltd, or GHL, is now an internationally renowned
organisation, whose founders have been involved in hovercraft design,
development, manufacturing and operation for over forty years. The
company has been awarded full Quality Assurance by the Ministry of
Defence, and is regularly certified by Lloyds Register of Shipping and
the US Coastguard, among others.

Today, GHL offers the world's largest range of hovercraft, and deals with customers across the globe. GHL's craft are so highly regarded they're used by the British Ministry of Defence, the Royal Marines, the Royal National Lifeboat Institution (RNLI), the Indian Coast Guard; the list goes on and on. Plus, these machines are relied upon in the harshest extremes of weather – exemplified by the United States Government who depended upon a 1500TD model for search and rescue missions in Antarctica.

Griffon Hovercraft Ltd now employs 45 personnel to continue to develop and innovate in the world of hovercraft. Among the extensive number of TD models, they have also produced an agricultural hovercraft and hovering cricket pitch covers for Lords and Old Trafford cricket grounds.

Interesting fact: The founders of Griffon Hovercraft Ltd made some of the very first experimental man-carrying hovercraft.

LTI (London Taxis International)

What they make: taxis
Founder: Robert 'Bobby' Jones
Founded: 1919
Based: Coventry, West Midlands
Number of staff: 450+

THOSE BLACK curves, that yellow beacon: saviour to uncountable inebriated travellers in the rain-drenched London night. Like the red telephone box, the black taxi is a true icon of London and Britain. The black taxi has always been manufactured in Coventry by LTI.

The origins of this most private form of public transport date back to the seventeenth century and the hackney carriage (a name still used today to officially describe London black cabs), which, coming from the French word *hacquenée* (translations vary but 'horse for hire' is widely regarded as accurate), was literally a horse-drawn coach. The term 'cab' comes from 'cabriolet', derived from the French for 'jump like a goat', which described the lighter, two-wheeled carriage that tended to bounce through the cobbled streets of London.

In 1919, Carbodies Ltd was established as a coach-building operation under the guidance of Robert 'Bobby' Jones on a small site on Old Church Road, Coventry. It was not long before the expanding

Images © LTI Limited reproduced with permission. Fairway and TX shape is a registered design. Fairway™, the TLI device, the LTI and the London Taxis International logos are all trademarks of LTI Limited

firm moved to new premises in West Orchard Street, followed by a further relocation to the present Holyhead Road factory in the mid 1920s. Carbodies soon gained a good reputation for fine-quality coach-building, and provided services to Daimler, Ford, Jaguar and Rolls-Royce, among other big names.

During World War Two, the factory produced a wide variety of vehicles and body shells, including a special mobile command post for Field Marshall Montgomery. But then, in the late 1940s, Carbodies diversified into building taxis. Contracts were negotiated between Carbodies, Mann & Overton and Austin Ltd to produce a number of prototype vehicles. The first FX3 taxi model, carrying the Austin badge, rolled off the production lines in 1948. During the next ten years, more than 7,000 taxis were produced, most of which were sold to the London market.

During the 1950s Carbodies produced bodies for the Commer van and (working with BSA) the body for the Daimler majestic. It also produced shells for every Ford convertible built until 1964. However, the demand for convertibles began to decline, and so

Carbodies concentrated more on making complete taxis.

In 1997 the name Carbodies was dropped in favour of London Taxis International.

LTI continue to innovate and push the design of the car forward whilst retaining its unmistakable shape. The current model, the TX4, has been given an overhaul; it is sleeker, more durable and environmentally friendly – the VM Motori R425 DOHC is the cleanest diesel engine ever to beat at the heart of a black taxi and has been built specifically to meet the latest Euro IV emissions legislation. In May 2007 the company produced its 2000th TX4 – the company has also signed a deal with Chinese firm Geely to start manufacturing the TX4 in Shanghai.

LTI have now produced over 100,000 taxis. So next time you hail a taxi on the streets of London and that shiny black hackney carriage comes your way, remember it was built in Coventry.

Interesting fact: Taxi drivers are not legally obliged to give change. If a large note is offered, the driver is entitled to take the cash and offer to post the change to the passenger's home address.

Morgan Motor Company Ltd

What they make:	cars
Founder:	H. F. S. Morgan
Founded:	Dates vary but 1910 is the first documented date.
Based:	Malvern, Worcestershire
Number of staff:	150

FEW HAVE made such an impact on the British car industry as one H. F. S. Morgan, and few have helped define the world car industry as significantly. As a journalist once said of a Morgan motor car, 'It is the first and last of the real sports cars.' The makers of the dream car, the creators of the most beautiful, elegant and fastest of machines are not Italian or American, but British.

Born in 1881 in Herefordshire, H. F. S. Morgan was a son of a clergyman, who quickly showed his potential at Crystal Palace engineering college before going on to work and learn under the tutelage of William Dean, chief engineer of the Great Western Railway. Perhaps it was his love of speed that pushed him away from the railways, but at the age of 25 he left to set up his own garage. Initially running buses, he became renowned for his special 10 hp, 15-seat Woseley bus. This gave him the financial power to buy his own three-wheeled Eagle Tandem. Unsatisfied with the performance, he set about making his own, and so the legendary Morgan car was born. The design was never intended to go into mass production, but was born out of inquisitiveness and the drive of an engineer determined to improve on what the supposed experts had already created.

Using the basic set-up of the Eagle, HFS took a 7 hp, twin-cylinder Peugeot engine and mounted it to a lightweight tubular chassis. Due to its rigid frame, lightweight and independent front suspension and the unusual power to weight ratio of 90 b.h.p. per tonne, it was able to accelerate as fast as any car being produced at the time. This is akin to an amateur creating a car with the performance of a Ferrari in his garage on his first attempt.

Morgan soon became an international player with their cars smashing through the records for speed, endurance and reliability. Within two years of production, Morgan had taken Britain and its motor industry onto the world stage and without the backing of multinational companies, world-class designers and engineers.

Morgan's early designs were so ahead of their time that few changes were needed for some years. All the while success on the racing circuits continued, so much so that in 1925 the Morgan car

entered in the Brooklands race had to start a whole lap behind the rest of the field to make the race more competitive. It still won.

There is now a one-year waiting list for any Morgan automobile; the Morgan owners club is gaining new members all the time and international markets are opening up as the Morgan brand flourishes around the world.

Interesting fact: The first two-seaters made their appearance at the 1911 Olympia Show. They were fitted with 8 hp engines. They attracted the interest of the managing director of Harrods, Mr Burbridge, and became the only car ever to appear in the shop window of the famous store.

Wit of
the Nation

Richard Benson

WIT OF THE NATION

Richard Benson

£9.99

Hardback

ISBN 13: 978 1 84024 620 9

'*Marriage is a very good thing, but I think it is a mistake to make a habit out of it*'
W. Somerset Maugham

'*What is a halo? It's only one more thing to keep clean*'
Christopher Fry

'*Thou hast no more brain than I have in mine elbows*'
William Shakespeare

Britain has long been littered with wicked wordsmiths of the highest calibre and what better way to celebrate all that makes Blighty brilliant than with this bumper book of witty one-liners?

With quips, quotes and insults from classic favourites William Shakespeare and Winston Churchill to modern masters John Cleese and Eddie Izzard, this delightful book will ensure you're never at a loss for the perfect witticism.

www.summersdale.com